Maria D' Andrea's
POSITIVELY POSITIVE SPELL BOOK
Vanquish All Negativity In Your Life And Put On A Happy Face

- EXCLUSIVE -
THE HISTORY OF PSYCHIC AND OCCULT ART IN AMERICA

Maria D' Andrea
With Additional Spells Offered By Dragonstar

MARIA D' ANDREA'S
POSITIVELY POSITIVE SPELL BOOK

Vanquish All Negativity In Your Life And Put On A Happy Face

By Maria D' Andrea
With Additional Spells Offered By
Dragonstar

Maria D' Andrea

MARIA D' ANDREA'S POSITIVELY POSITIVE SPELL BOOK

Vanquish All Negativity In Your Life
And Put On A Happy Face

By Maria D' Andrea
With Additional Spells Offered By
Dragonstar

**Copyright © 2015 - Global Communications/Inner Light Publications
dba Timothy Green Beckley
All Rights Reserved**

Printed in the United States of America

No part of this book may be reproduced, stored in retrieval system or transmitted in any form by any means, electronic, mechanical, photocopying, recording or otherwise without the express permission of the publisher. Please address any questions about this book to: mrufo8@hotmail.com

Timothy Green Beckley: Editorial Director

Carol Ann Rodriguez: Publishers Assistant

Tim R. Swartz: Editor

Sean Casteel: Associate Editor

William Kern: Associate Editor

Cover Graphics: Tim R. Swartz

For Free Subscription to The Conspiracy Journal Write:
Global Communications
Box 753, New Brunswick, NJ 08903

Email: mrufo8@hotmail.com

www.ConspiracyJournal.Com
www.TeslasSecretLab.Com

TO THOSE THAT HAVE HELPED ME LEAD A POSITIVE LIFE, I DEDICATE THIS WORK

I dedicate this book to my loving family:

To both my sons Rick and Rob who are spiritual, always supportive and adventurous at heart. They are my inspiration.

My son Rob D'Andrea is an entrepreneur, courageous and smart.

My son Rick Holecek is knowledgeable, fearless and a seeker.

His wife Gina who has diligence and focus. They are the essence of family.

To their children Ryan and Cara who are always loving and intelligent.

To Timothy Green Beckley who is not only my publisher, but my great friend for many years.

And finally to Tim Swartz and fellow psychic Dragonstar for their help in my endeavors.

Indeed, I truly feel Blessed.

Maria

November 2015

THE IMPORTANCE OF ENGAGING IN POSITIVE OCCULT SPELLS

An Introduction For Aspiring To The Good Life

By Maria D'Andrea

EVERYTHING that we do, say, think and fell has an effect on the universe. It is mind power. When we send negative thoughts thowards someone - yes even thoughts! - if their aura is open to the negativity, it will have a negative effect on them. However, if their aura is closed and protected, the negativity will bounce off their aura and be returned to the sender.

On the other hand, if we send positive, loving thoughts towards others who are receptive to such positive feelings, there will be a positive effect on their life.

Like begets like in everyday life and especially in an individual's occult work. If the individual is not receptive, is closed to positive vibrations, then the positive feelings will rebound back to the sender. An actual spell would be a more intense way of sending out either positive or negative thoughts to cause an effect.

You will always be better off trying to send positive energy through positive spells. This way all that exists around you and your loved ones, - i.e. friends and family – will benefit in a completely positive, beneficial, way. It's a format, I find, that never fails.

And that my friend is the overall purpose of this book - to teach you how to create a positive universe for yourself and thus benefit all around from a lack of negativity in your life.

This is why dear friends I wanted so much to write this book.

I decided to write this book to inspire you to have not only abundance in all its forms, but so you can sing in harmony with the vibrations of life. Dance under the stars or bright sunshine and feel happier.

Magick is all around you. It is like a radio station and I am here to help you tune in on the right frequency.

This book is meant to help you to gain control over the direction you are heading toward. You are a powerful force of Mother Nature, you just need the right tools to awaken.

My earlier life was very difficult, but I was always positive and psychic which helped me. I came over during the Hungarian Revolution and for many years it still continued to be a difficult path, for various reasons. But I stay positive because that is my nature, and I know that we can always create a joyous future. We have the ability.

I truly believe in Karmic Law which states that whatever you do comes back to you; good, bad or indifferent. There is also an Occult (metaphysical) Law that says-"Like Attracts Like." So be conscious of the people around you so they are positive and supportive, and you have to keep guard over your thoughts. To work magick and have it succeed, you must have an intent, strong focus, and strong desire. Without those qualities, the magickal techniques won't work. Even then, the energies of the universe can play havoc. Sometimes you receive what is best for you, not exactly what your intent was focused upon. As to the emotional charge- if you are neutral or don't care, why would the universal energies?

Remember YOU are a Spiritual Warrior. We are all connected, dancing in the Light of the Cosmos. Weaving our Paths and futures and intertwining with all forces of nature. As a shaman, our outlook is to think of a spider web made of White Light and think of each soul of a person on one of the threads. When one person moves, it shakes the whole web.

I'm excited to help you bring about a positive, prosperous life. I only write positive books because the thoughts we have now will create our future. Once you step off the Path of Light you are creating negativity in your life at some point. I am helping others to not only have a better life, but to have fun doing so.

These techniques are to be taken seriously, with respect and focus. However, that doesn't mean we have to be serious all the time. We are all meant to be happy and have fun. In fact our sense of humor, as you will find, is a little different. After all, if we can change things, how upset can we really be long term?

The reason I teach classes and am a public speaker on the Spiritual/Psychic/Metaphysical/Paranormal Fields is so everyone can find joy. In fact, I have some of my TV shows on YouTube-"The Spiritual World With Maria," where I also teach.

If you find yourself angry, upset, sad or dwelling on the negatives in your life (we've all had those times), simply repeat the word "cancel" several times and rephrase it to the opposite. You don't need to believe it, but the universe is very technical and will "hear" the direction you are now creating and will help to get you there. Also keep an eye out for opportunities because you don't know how your outcome will manifest.

Many people focus on negativity such as is found in some books, media, and newspapers among other situations. That doesn't uplift you or give you the power to change things for the better. How much better do you feel when you are around positive, supportive, happy, like-minded people?

Take back your Inner Power and change / improve your life to be what you visualize it to be. You are a child of Divine Power and so do not have any limitations. If you can think it, you can create it. Do not misunderstand the timing with the outcome. Look at all the people who achieved at so many different.

Go outside, look at the beautiful stars and relax. Be inspired. Dance in the moonlight. Then go and change your life....And practice only positive magick!

In any occult work it is necessary to utilize certain spiritual components like candles, incense, oils, herbs, talismans, parchment, gemstones and crystals, and even to build your own simple alter on which to work your spells.

Most of the items mentioned throughout this text can be easily found locally, or I suggest contacting AzureGreen Occult Supplies at P.O. Box 48, middlefield, MA 01243.

You might want to ask me as well as I may have some of what you will need to do your best occult work.

A SPELL TO ATTRACT OTHERS

Your spiritual tools are:

A Pink candle

Violet or Lavender Oil

6 Sunflower Leaves or Rose Petals

Place the flower petals or leaves around the base of the candle. Anoint the candle with one of the oils and as it burns chant three times with focus and sincerity:

Come to me my new found friends,

Come to me from everywhere,

From high and low,

From near and far,

With loving hearts and thoughts like mine.

Let the candle burn out on its own.

Pick up the petals or leaves one at a time. As you do this, with each petal or leaf - Focus on "seeing" laughing, happy new friends coming to your door who have the outlook on life that you have. "See" yourself happy to welcome them into your home. Consciously think of how you will feel when they arrive, such as: glad, excited, energetic. Each night before sleep, get a feeling of excitement as you expect their arrival.

Place the petals or leaves in any container near your front door.

Throw the candle away outside of your home.

A SPELL TO DEAL BETTER WITH CHANGE

Be more flexible and deal much better with changes in your life. Some changes are positive but still may be difficult to adapt to, some are hard to deal with but it need to be dealt with so you can feel better, have more harmony within yourself and adjust to individual situations better.

Get a white candle and lemon oil. If you cannot find lemon oil, squeeze some (1/8 t. will do) lemon juice into some (about ¼ c.) olive oil.

The white candle keeps the spell positive and the lemon oil is for power.

Rub the oil on the top including the wick and the sides of the candle. Next, light it.

As you do this, say out loud, with conviction 3 times:

Candle, candle burning bright,

Let me see my way with light,

As this candle flickers out,

My changes all I can surmount.

When the candle burns to the bottom, take a little piece of it when cooled off to carry with you.

Each time you feel the difficulty with changes, touch the candle piece to help you become more flexible and make the changes easier.

Next, take the rest of the burned candle and throw it away outside your home.

BE PROTECTED WHILE IN A MOVING VEHICLE

In this day and age, car safety is very important.

This spell changes improves situations as much as possible. For example: If you are in a bad neighborhood and someone wishes to steal your car, they will still steal a car because we can't change who they are, but it will not be yours; If someone had a car accident, it would be less catastrophic than it would have been with less or no physical harm.

Get a Clear Quartz Crystal and leave it in direct sunlight for 3 days to cleanse all negative energy that may be within it. The size of the Crystal doesn't matter because it works on vibration.

Get a small pouch of any color or make your own. Place 3 Tablespoons of Lavender in it, and close the pouch with 3 knots. If you are making your own, then sew up all the sides once you place the herb into the center.

Now hold both the Crystal and the Lavender Pouch in between your cupped hands and say with intent, as a Command (this is not a request):

I now Invoke the Power of the Universe, Divine Power, and all Positive Forces of Protection to keep safe my car or wherever these tools of Power are placed.

And so it is.

Now place them anywhere in y our car and leave them there.

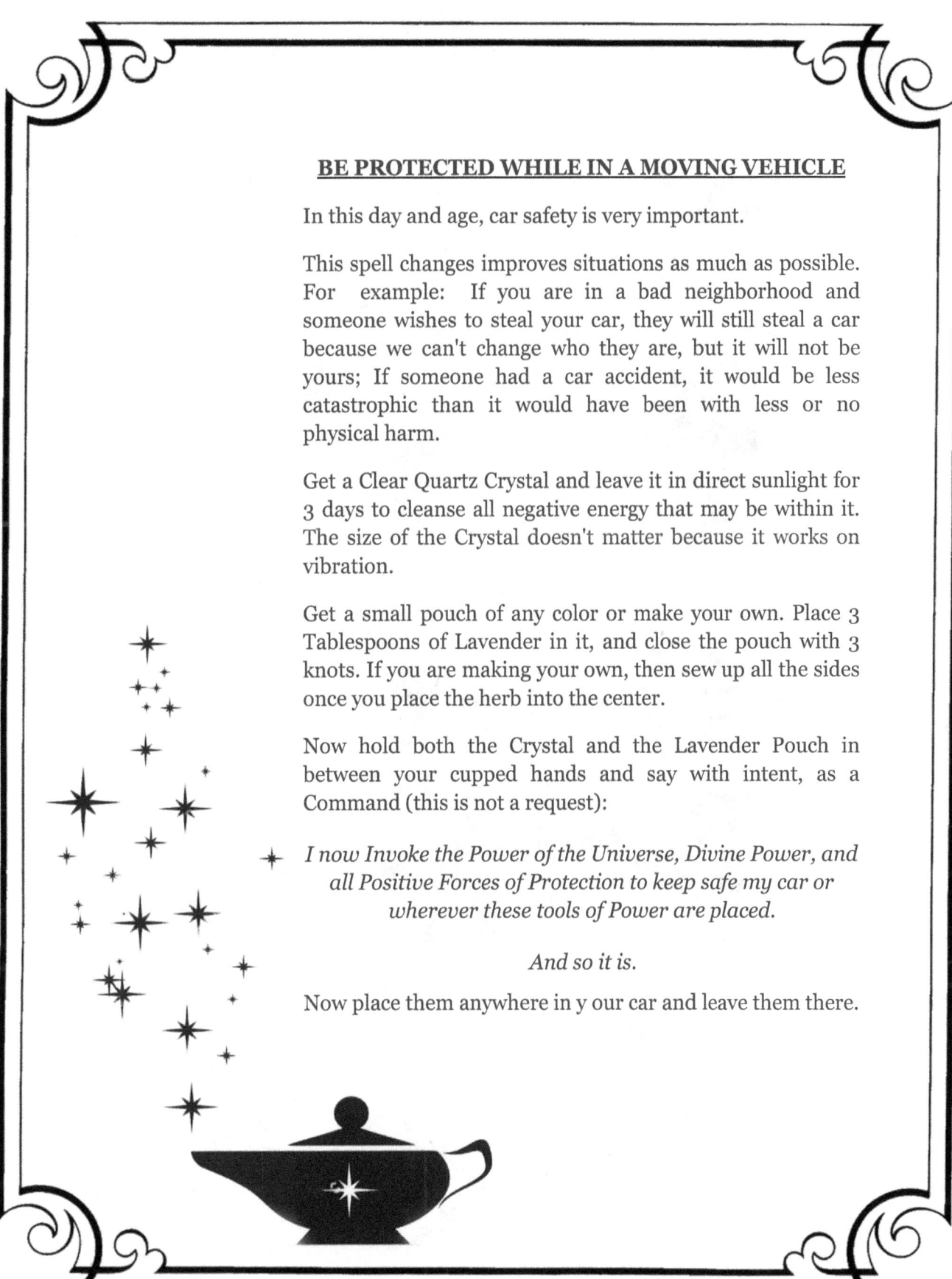

TO BREAK A HEX

Tools:

A Lily - you only need part of the flower

1 Bay Leaf

3 Garlic Cloves

Some Parsley- about 4 Tablespoons dried or a small fresh bunch.

1 Tigers Eye Stone of any size.

A White Pouch.

Sandalwood Incense.

Place all ingredients except the incense into the pouch and tie it closed with 5 knots.

Wear something white or have a white handkerchief or cloth on you.

Light the incense and as it starts to smoke, hold the pouch over it and invoke with focus:

As I say, so shall it be,

Protection Power comes to me,

Fire bright and air of light,

Break this hex of evil might.

Place the pouch over the entry door to your home. When the incense burns out, sprinkle it outside all entry to your home.

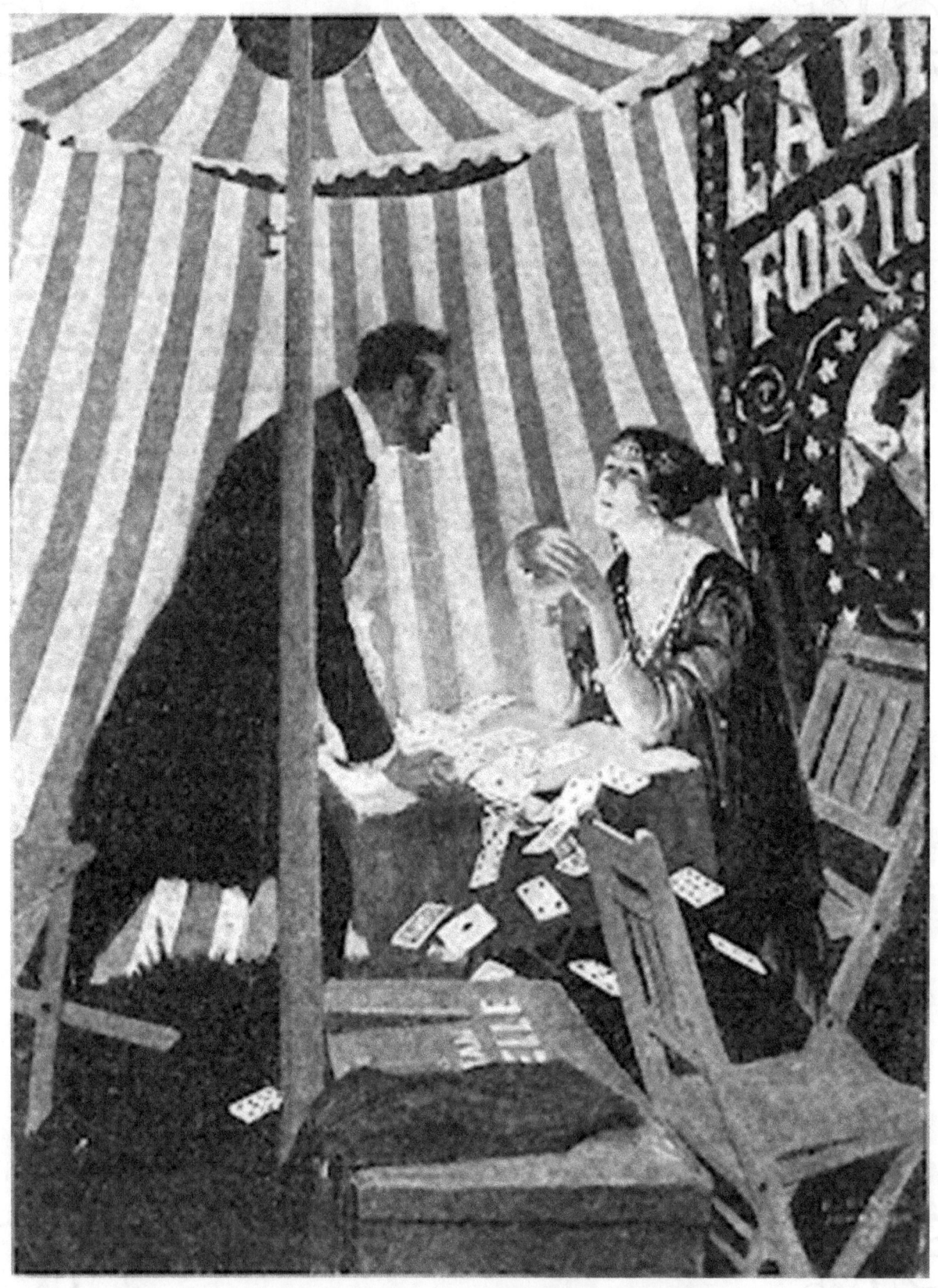

I CALL IT "TIGER LUCK"

Bring the luck of the powerful tiger to you.

Increase your luck by carrying 3 Job's tears (also known as Coix Seed).

Brew some Chamomile tea and place the Job's tears into it for 7 days. Take them out of the tea and dry them off. Take the tea and wash your hands in it then throw it away inside your home to keep the energy.

Hold the Job's tears between your cupped hands at the next New Moon. Focus on "seeing" yourself in lucky situations.

While holding them, incant:

Tiger in the morning light,

Bring to me what I desire,

Luck abounds and comes to me,

From air and earth,

From fire and sea.

Luck of power comes to me,

As I say so shall it be.

Carry the Job's tears with you in your pocket or pocketbook, keeping it within three feet of your body.

MONEY MAGICK IS A NECESSITY

Get a clear jar with a top that closes. With a gold colored magic marker, paint or crayon, draw a circle on the side of the jar and an 8.

On a white paper with black ink, write the following at the top:

Through Divine Power

In a Perfect Way

This or Better

Then write the amount of money you have as your goal for this month or this year. Be specific about the time and amount.

Next, drop 8 coins of any denomination into the jar one at a time. As each coin drops, say with intent:

Coins of silver, coins of gold,

Paper money that unfolds,

Come to me with swiftest wings,

Place the jar where you can see it daily but where visitors, negative people or jealous people will not see your jar.

Each day put some money into it and "see" it overflow.

Not only are you showing expansion but you will be surprised how money comes to you in different ways.

When the jar is full, empty it and start again with the 8 coins.

BLESSINGS FOR ALL YOUR LOVELY PETS

This ritual can also be performed for pets/animals at a distance. Your pet does not have to be there or you may want to do this spell for a friends pet.

As an example: This can be for a dog, cat, fish, horse or any animal.

Do this consecration on a Friday or Sunday.

Take a photo of your pet / animal and go outside or next to an open window with it.

Hold the picture in your hand.

Looking at the picture Say:

Gods and Goddesses of the Light,

Bless and Protect (name of pet) throughout

his/her life,

Keep him/her happy, safe from harm,

Bless (name of pet) with a joyful life.

Thank You

Take the picture and burn it to ashes. You may need to relight it a few times till it is all ash.

Take the ashes outside and throw them to the wind, so they are carried to the realm of the Gods and Goddesses. As you do so, thank them again.

Psychic Readings
Palm | Tarot | Crystal Ball

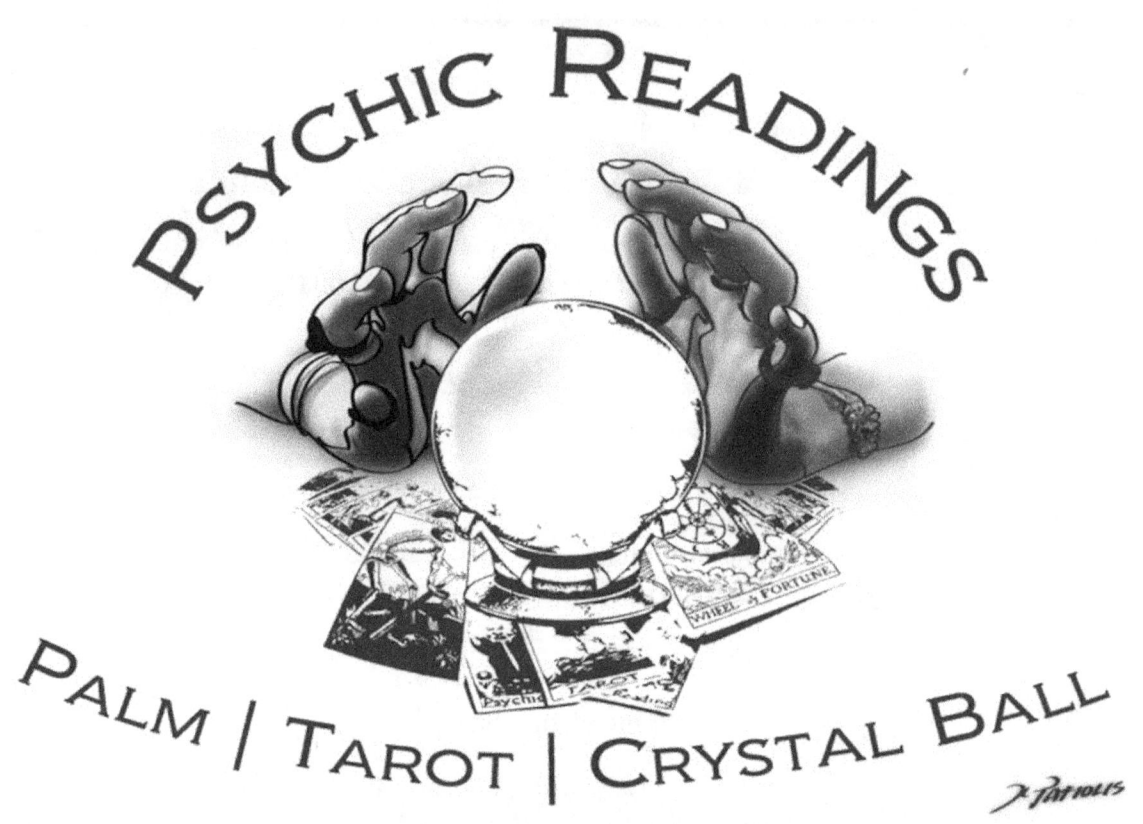

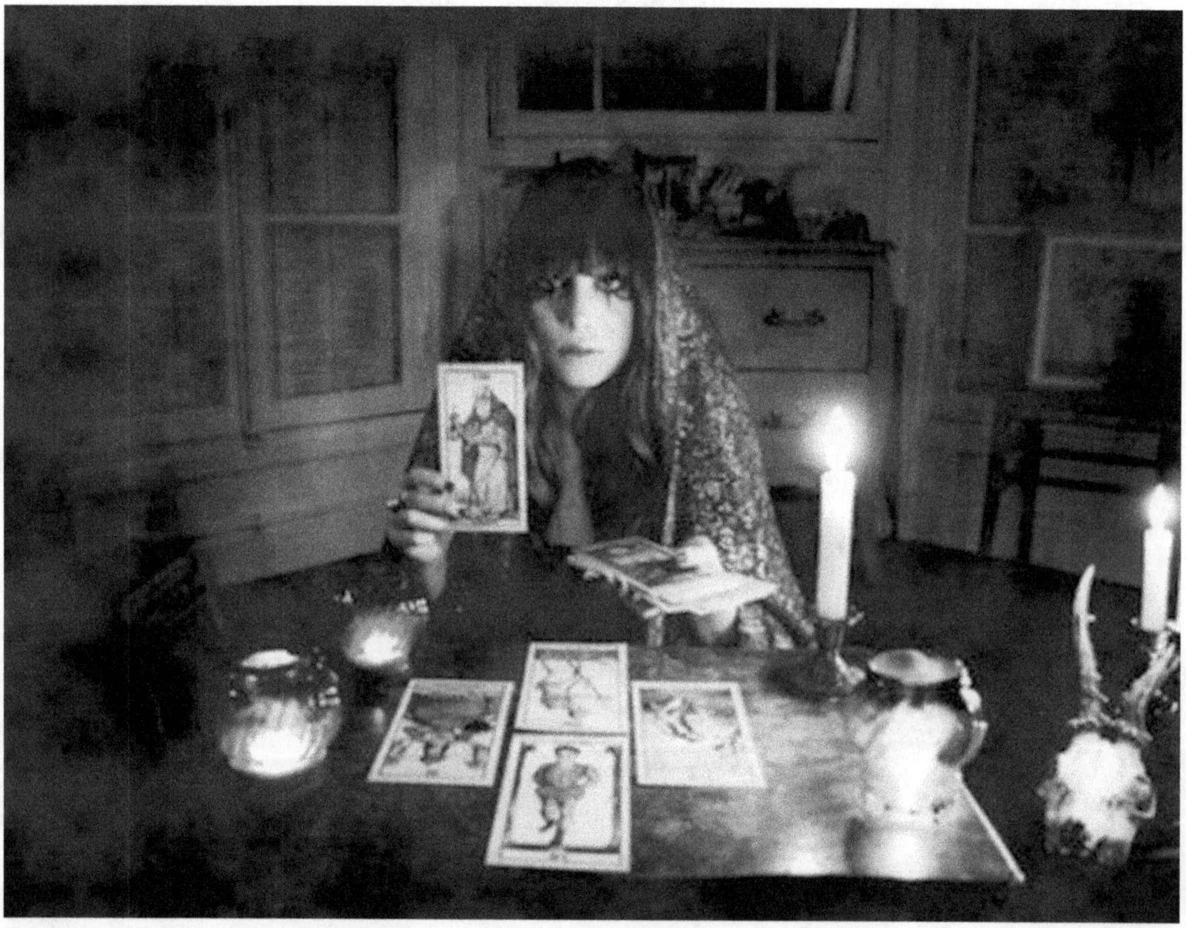

NEPTUNE'S FREEDOM GAINING SPELL

At times we are in situations where we feel limited, controlled, where we feel we do not have inner freedom.

This spell is to create a better situation and have you obtain freedom.

Do this ritual at a Full moon.

Get a bowl of water filled to the brim.

Add 1 drop of eucalyptus oil.

Drop 5 bay leaves into the bowl.

Under it place a picture of yourself happy, smiling, in a good mood.

Look into the water as you focus and say:

> *Neptune's might I now invoke,*
>
> *To free me from this dreadful yoke,*
>
> *Wash away this darkness now,*
>
> *Nothing holds me from now on.*
>
> *Freedom, freedom,*
>
> *You are mine,*
>
> *Neptune's might has overcome.*

Throw the water away outside and place your happy picture where you will see it every day. If you don't want to leave it out, place it on top of your things in a drawer you open each day.

HUNGARIAN (MAGYAR) GARDEN BLESSING

We Bless our gardens for protection, growing beautiful flowers, food for animals and big tasty vegetables, among other reasons.

My mother had a green thumb and loved the outdoors. She treated them with love and they overdid themselves for her.

When you work with nature, remember we are all connected energetically on this planet. Treat your Plant Kingdom with love and respect and you will be surprised how well they do.

Take a container of any size of milk and add some honey, 6 bay leaves and sugar.

** If you are consecrating indoor plants, do so with a container of water with 6 bay leaves in it.

Walk the garden sprinkling some of the blend as you say and repeat:

You are Blessed. You are Protected. You are Loved.

You are Healed. You are Safe. You are Loved.

Take what is left of the water if any and pour it into the earth.

Each day talk to your garden with caring.

Remember to weed and take care of it.

Thank the garden for being bountiful. (Or whatever word you are comfortable with.)

PSYCHIC / INTUITIVE VISION QUEST

Do this with a serious mind set only. Gather together the following:

1- A purple candle

2- The dried herb known as mugwort

3- Dark purple cloth

4- Bowl to burn the mugwort

Place the cloth on a clean, cleared spot. It can be an altar, the top of a dresser, or anywhere convenient without anything else on it.

Place the bowl on the center of the cloth.

Place the purple candle directly across from you, behind the bowl.

Put some of the mugwort in the bowl. For Protection FIRST say:

Divine Power Protect Me.

Light the dried herb and let the smoke permeate around you. As you say:

Visions come and carry me accurately and safely.

I am open ONLY to positive.

I am open as long as it does not hurt my

Mind, Body and Soul.

So Be It.

Then allow yourself to close your eyes, relax, breathe slowly and be aware of what comes to you. It takes patience. ALWAYS protect yourself first.

THE MAGICK OF LOVE

Love magick is not controlling. It is meant to make both of you happy. To bring in new love or heighten the love you have already with your partner do the following spell.

Do this ritual on a Friday.

In a quiet room, place 4 pink candles at each cardinal point. (East, West, North, South) Use a compass if possible, otherwise as close as you can get to these directions.

You are the center point standing in the middle.

Face the East first and light this candle.

Next light the South candle.

Light the candle to the West next.

Last light the North candle.

Repeat 3 times with feeling and expectancy:

Love by magick come to me,

Bring us perfect harmony.

Go about your daily business and keep an eye open for new situations. If you are already with someone, this will make you closer.

Then let the candles burn out by themselves. Once out, throw them away outside.

Always keep an open heart and open mind.

SUCCESS IN BUSINESS

Write the name of your business / job / place of employment on a white paper with black ink.

Take the paper and place it under a green candle.

Place coins around the base of the candle.

Light the green candle and focus on all your business goals for a minute.

Next, with your eyes closed, visualize your business/job, 1st as it is right now. Then with a red crayon in your mind, put a big red X over it.

Then as step 2, visualize the business/job situation the same as your goal once it is achieved surrounded by bright gold light. See it, feel it. Sense it. KNOW that it is already in the process of success.

How would you feel once you had this goal? Let yourself physically smile. Enjoy your achievement.

 *** Important- each day, wake up and expect your goal to be there. Look for it. Sometimes opportunities come in to help you to advance toward it. Pay attention and look for these and move on them.

Let the candle burn out and bury it along with the paper outside.

Take the coins and carry them with you.

Keep yourself focused and in a positive mood.

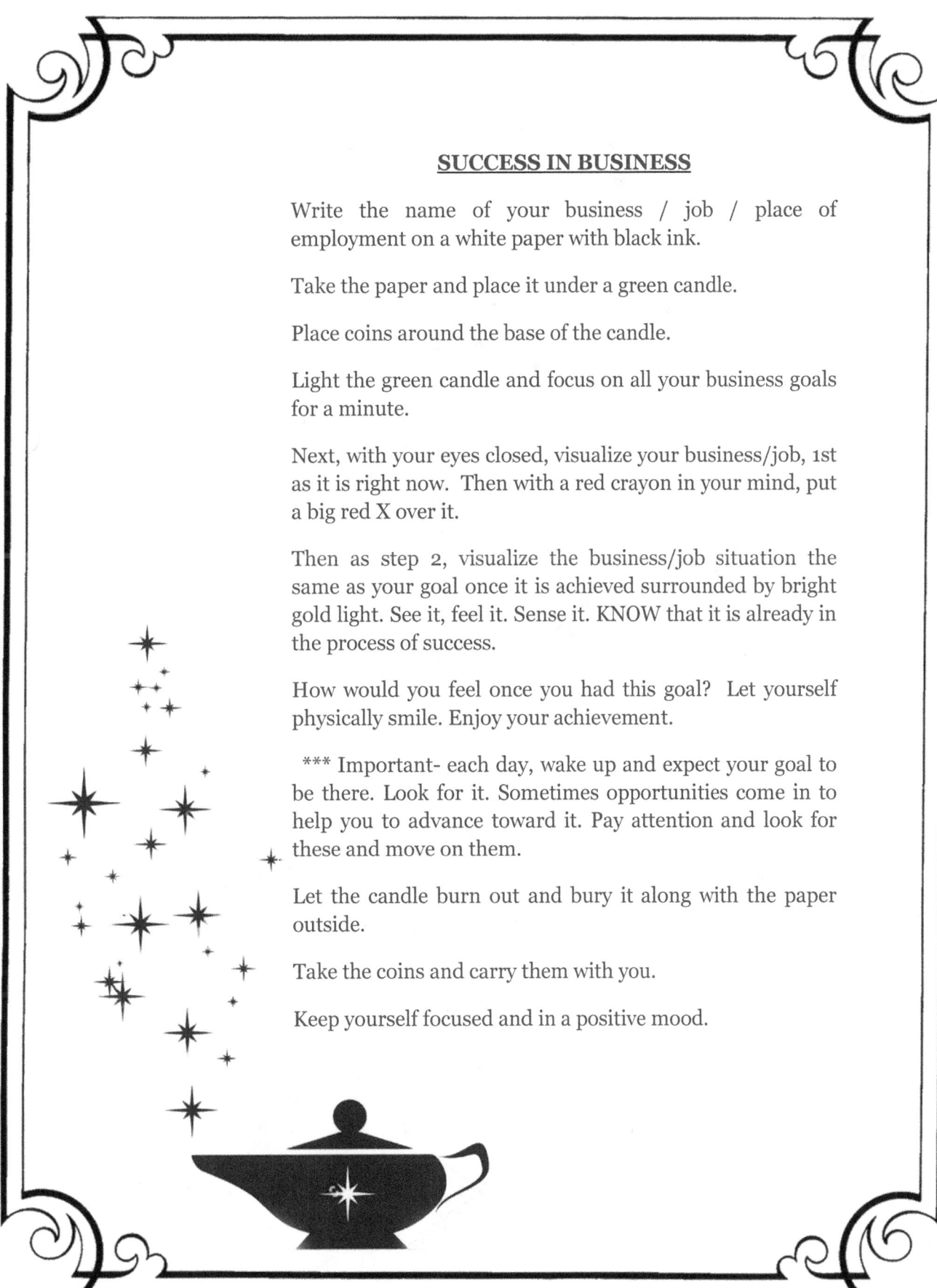

TROUBLE RELEASING SPELL

First find a stick of wood that will float in water. The length or width does not matter.

Next, focus on what troubles you. It can be one single situation or several situations.

Utilizing sympathetic magic:

With a knife, carve symbols into the stick to represent each of your problems. As you do this, focus on what the troubles are.

Sprinkle some of the herb known as mint over it.

Go to the ocean, lake or any body of water. Hold the wood in your hands and with sincerity say these Words of Power:

Peace and harmony come to me,

Troubles now go into the sea,

To the bottom they must go,

Never to surface as I Let Go.

As I say, so shall it be,

Into the depth of the deep blue sea.

Take the wood and place it into the water giving it a little push to move it on its way. Turn around, don't look back and walk away.

KNOW that all your troubles are now leaving and are being replaced with peace, harmony, relief and joy.

REAP AMAZING PROSPERITY

As a shaman, I make medicine bags individually for each person. However, there are some we can blend for everyone. Remember, your intent is also a powerful tool that has to be added as you do your magickal work.

Tools of magick:

2 Lodestones

2 Tonka Beans

Piece of a pine tree (bark, needles or any part)

1 Turquoise stone

Orange pouch or bag (medicine bag)

Peony Oil

Place the lodestone, Tonka beans, pine and turquoise into the orange pouch.

Anoint the medicine bag with Peony Oil by putting a drop on your finger and drawing the symbol of a circle with a dot in the center on it. This is an alchemy symbol for the sun and success.

As you do so, focus on success coming to you in all forms and visualize yourself feeling happy and excited.

Tie the medicine bag closed with 3 knots.

Carry this medicine bag with you no farther than 3 feet away from your body. At night, sleep with it nearby.

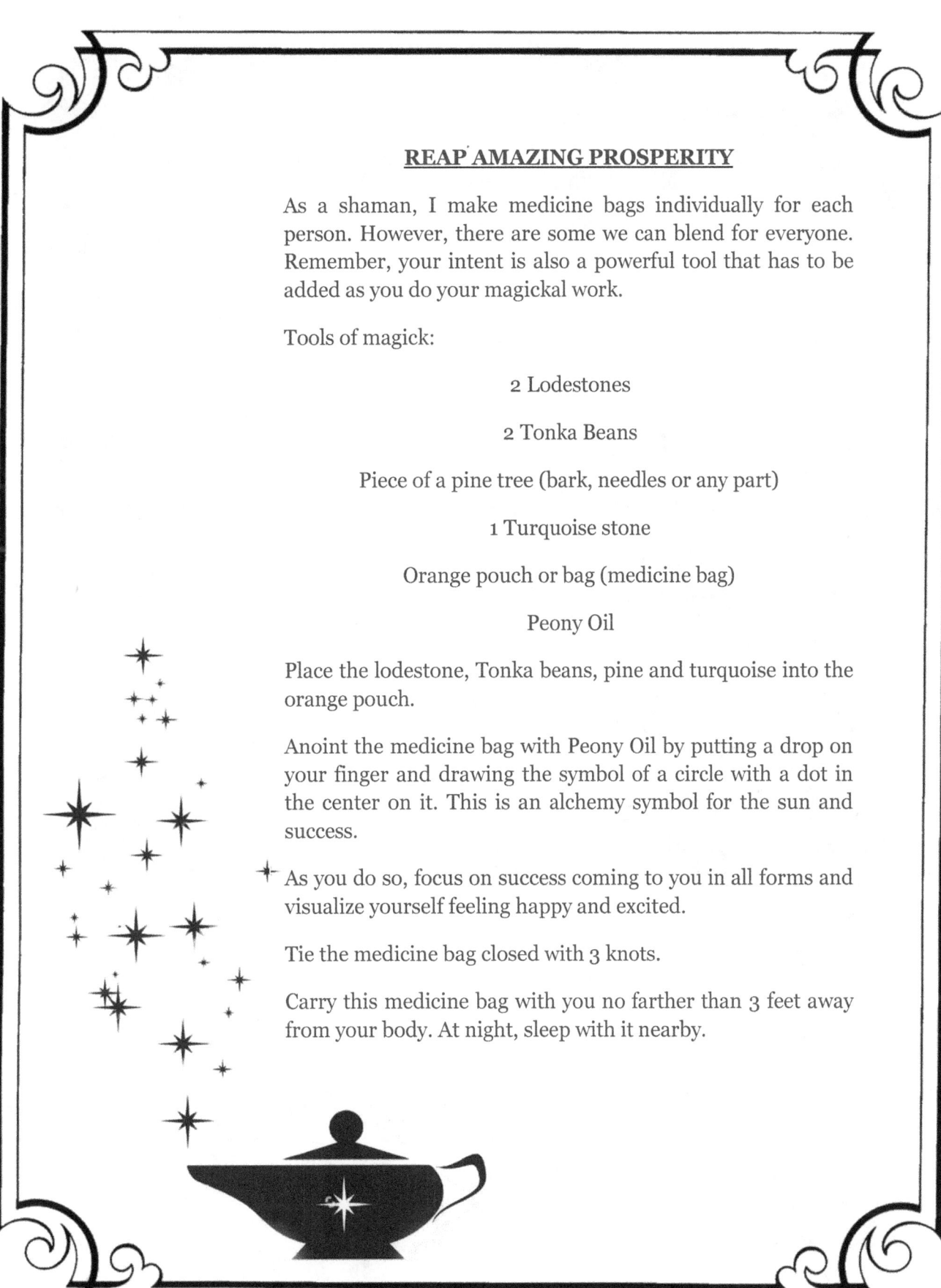

SPIRIT RAINBOW HEALING

Throughout many years, I've worked with several forms of healing. I eventually originated a healing modality that is powerful and I call it the "Spirit Rainbow Healing System". Several of my students now also teach my technique.

This is a small easy part that you can utilize to speed up your natural healing process.

Get a green light bulb and sit under this light for 20 minutes at a time. * Not more at one time! (Option- You can do this several times a day.)

As you do so, do the following for a few minutes:

Place one hand on the area that needs the healing.

Place your other hand on the opposite spot on your body that is the farthest from your first hand.

Visualize the color pink flowing from one hand to the other, back and forth throughout your body. See it whirling around you and permeating through you. Visualize gray spots where your body needs the increased healing. Next, see the pink color swallowing the gray and replacing it with beautiful, clear pink.

Next, add in the color green and run that through your body and see it whirling around you. In a bright, clear green.

See your body perfectly healthy, all the cells and molecules clear and healthy. Do this for a few minutes. Then relax.

On a piece of paper write "I have perfect health" and tape it on a container of water for 48 hours. (You can refrigerate it.) Then drink it.

ODIN'S TRAVEL SAFETY

When you travel, Odin will keep you and your belongings safe.

First, on white paper with red ink, write the capital letter R. Place this with your luggage or any travel items. This ensures that they do not get lost or misplaced. If rarely they do, they will be found and returned to you.

Prior to traveling, work this spell every day for a week.

Make a tea from mint leaves. You can utilize a tea bag, but cut it open and only use the leaves. If you leave it in the pouch, it changes the vibration due to the paper and glue or staple holding the string or bag together.

Let this tea steep for at least 20 minutes. Wash your hands with it and repeat this invocation 3 times:

Odin, I now invoke your Protection in my

travels to (fill in your destination) until I

return safely home.

After you have repeated the above 3 times, say:

And this is so. Thank you Odin.

Take the remaining tea and throw it away outside.

VICTORY CAN BE YOURS!

There are many forms of victory such as: emotional, physical, mental, spiritual. Focus your intent on your specific situation when you call for victory.

In a handkerchief of white or a pouch, carry the following:

    1 High John The Conqueror Root

    1 Tiger Eye Stone

    1 Turquoise stone

    1 pair of lodestones

Tie this closed with 1 knot.

Burn Frankincense incense and as the smoke rises, hold the pouch over it and chant:

Victory, victory, victory mine,

Aided by the Powers Divine,

Bring to me what I desire,

Light my way with Heavenly fire.

Carry the pouch with you.

When the incense burns out, throw it away inside your home so you do not cancel this spell.

ANTI-STRESS SPIRITUAL BATH

When you take a spiritual bath, also known as an immersion bath, you fill the bathtub with water high enough to reach your neck.

Do not use soap or any other product at this time because it will change the vibration of the water and will cancel the effect.

Take this time to shut off phones, TV, radio or any other disturbances.

Make a tea with the herb called thyme.

Fill your bathtub and add this tea to the water.

Either immerse your whole body in the water for a second when you first get in or before you get into the water splash some water on your face and head.

Spend at least 20 minutes soaking. Think only positive thoughts. These could be prayers, a vacation you wish to go on at some point, a happy past experience or a future one you would like to have. Anything positive will do. If you find yourself thinking of something less positive, such as bills you need to pay, simply refocus on a positive thought.

When you are finished with your Spiritual bath, allow yourself to air dry if possible.

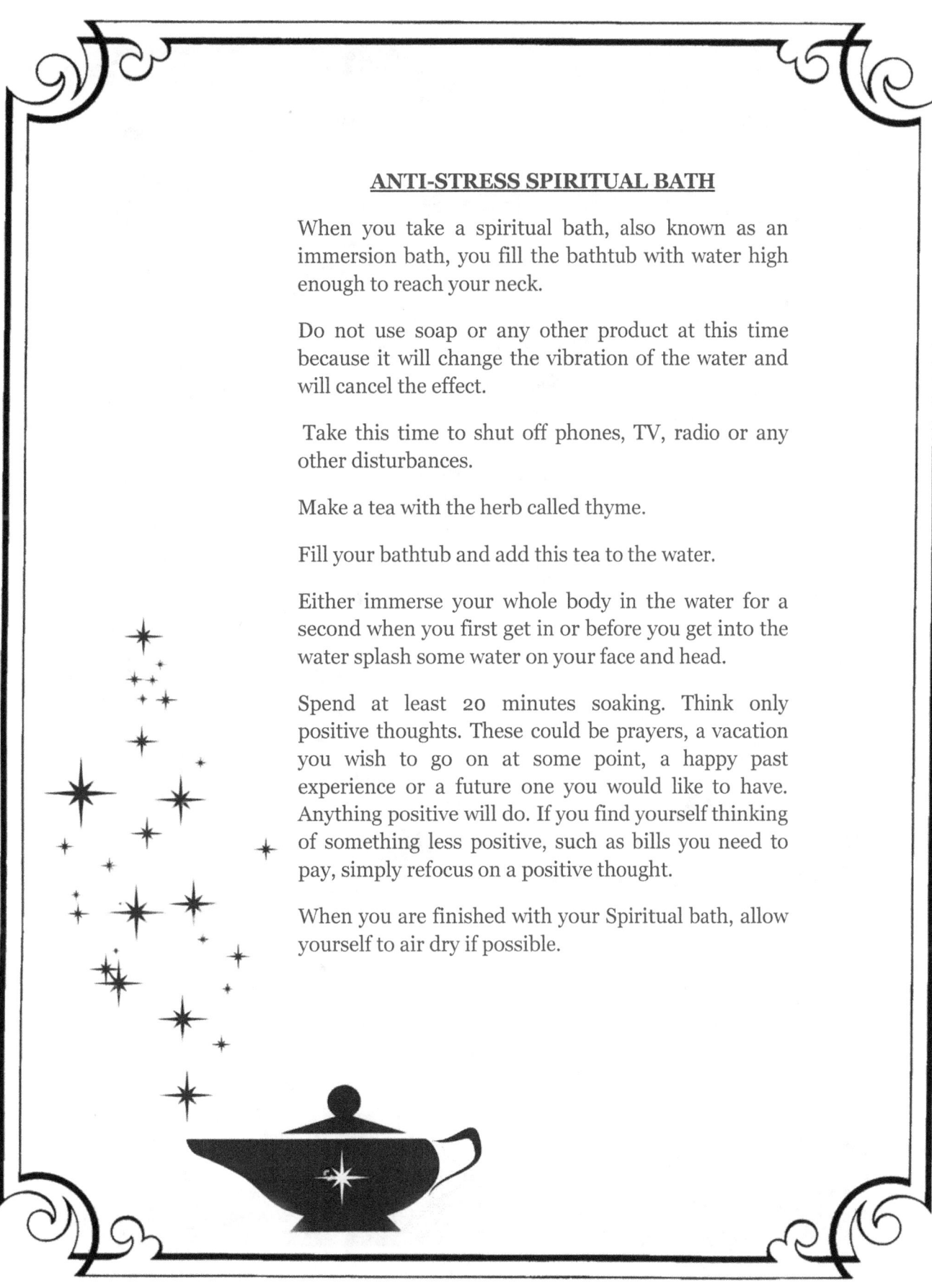

COMPUTER PROTECTION

This spell is twofold. 1- It helps protect the computer. 2- It protects you from all negative electrical energies.

Place clear quartz crystals next to your computer, screen, fax, printer and any other devices connected to your computer.

Once every 6 months, place them overnight in a bowl of water with a Tablespoon of sea salt. Then dry them off in the morning and place them back in the spots.

Hold either hand above the computer and call on Mercury, the God of communication:

Mercury now come to me,

Earth and fire, air and sea,

Protection I now seek from thee,

Safely surround this tool for me.

And as I speak, so it shall be.

The word "tool" is used to cover all the software and hardware, and any part we may not consciously think about, so nothing is left out and we do not need to make a long list or do each one individually.

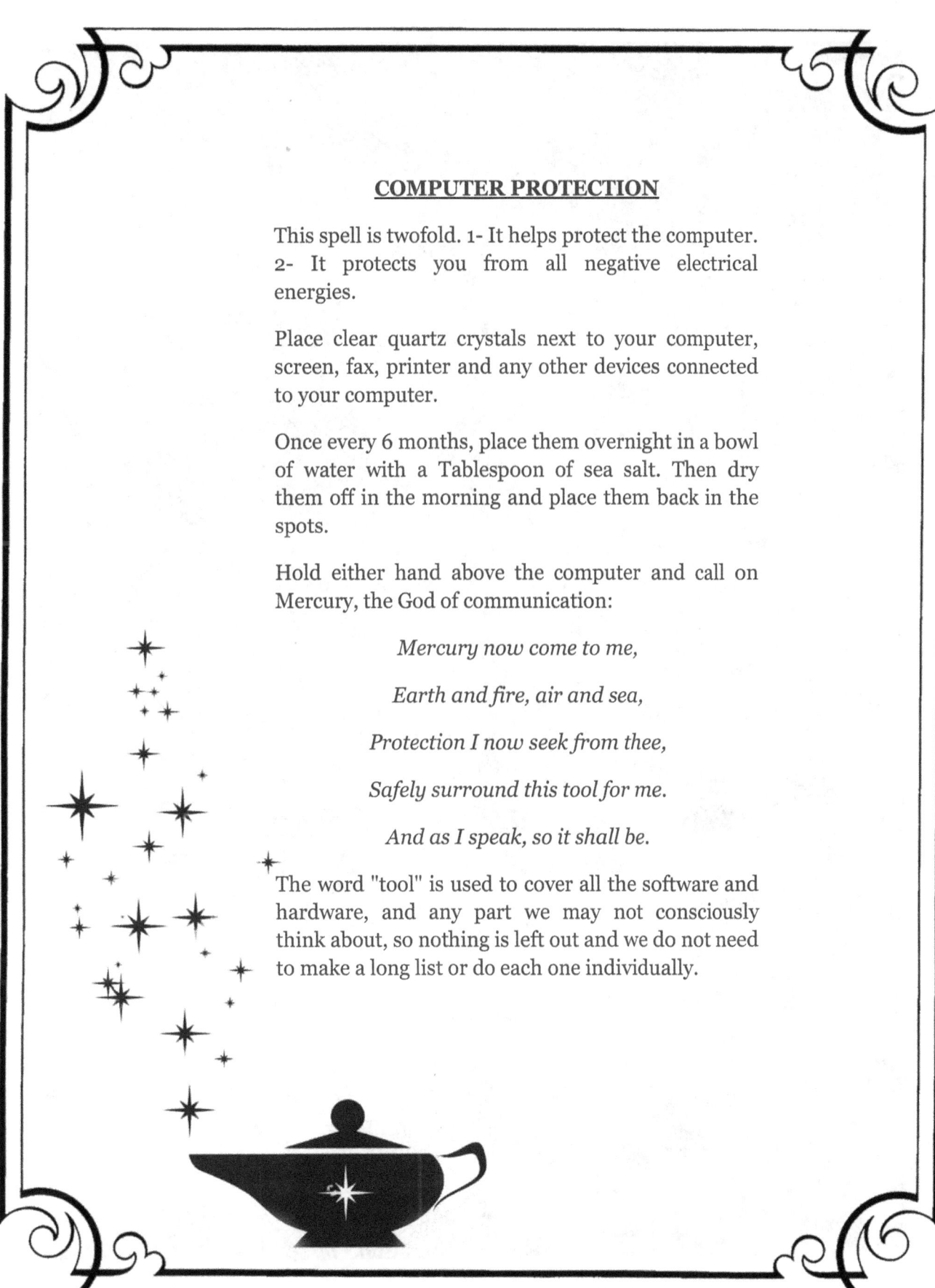

A SPECIAL HOUSE CLEANSING

Take a broom and you will start from the walls toward the center of each room on each floor of your home. It cannot be made of other materials. It has to be made from "broom".

Focus on all negative energy leaving your home and going back to nature to be cancelled out.

Sweep toward the center and incant as a command (you are not asking a request, you are making a statement / command with force):

Negativity dark and cold,

Leave my home to Light and warmth,

In the Power of Divine,

I command you leave this spot.

When you get to the center, sweep it outside and visualize it leaving or just KNOW that it has. Do not take it from room to room before sending it out the door, because this will build the negativity as it is added together.

When you are finished with all the rooms, make sure you say Thank You to Divine Power for the help. This is an important last step.

MORE POSITIVE SPELLS FROM THE SAGE KNOWN AS DRAGONSTAR
Continue forthright...

MAGICK AS A WAY OF LIFE
By Dragonstar

WE are children of the universe. Made from space dust that was swirling in space long before the earth or the solar system was formed. This is why the movement of planets can have an effect on people's emotions. Just as the moon and its monthly cycles affects the tidal seas and the life of all plants and animals.

It has been observed that when a person thinks and feels lucky, then that person will actually begin to attract luck. The fact that so many rich and successful people own and believe in charms, seems to support this theory. However, is it simply belief, or can it actually be mind over matter at work?

According to Stephen Michael Nanninga, in our modern age, the value of metaphysics is not generally taken seriously within the scientific community. This is understandable. The practice of philosophizing physical theory has no place in conventional science where theories and ideas must remain just that until verified objectively. However, as we come to understand what metaphysics actually is, we begin to realize that modern physics is metaphysics in a rediscovered and more perfected form.

Conventional science, the objectively knowable perspective on reality, and the entire Universe it describes, become recognized as expressions of a transcendental state of reality which, by virtue of its unchangeable unified condition, is even more real than the physical Universe itself.

The purpose of metaphysics is often misunderstood among religious thinkers. When a teaching becomes so dogmatic that it loses track of any sort of metaphysical understanding of the transcendental omnipresence, it becomes essentially stagnant and blind to what a spiritual universe is all about. Those familiar with the mystical philosophies of magick do not have a problem with the abstract universal principles of metaphysics and how they relate to the restrictions of theological traditions. Ideally, the ultimate goal of any theological tradition should be to bring the individual seeker to a state of spiritual awareness in which all such theological traditions are assimilated, and at the same time, not needed in their dogmatic form.

Much has been written in recent years about the enlightening parallels between modern physical theory and ancient metaphysics. Not only is science finding it increasingly difficult to keep itself separated from philosophical speculation, but as we develop our abstract understanding of the universe as a whole, the fields of physics and metaphysics seem to be losing their distinction altogether.

More than ever, as we examine our field of space-time from every possible perspective, we probe our consciousness for the mystical truth. With our great pride in scientific knowledge, have we ignorantly filed the most beautiful principles of ancient mysticism into the category of the absurd? In our secular materialism and religious zeal, have we forgotten the real substance of the ancient message?

Have we forgotten the true meaning of reality? Yet, perhaps we are not so lost after all. Perhaps we are at the dawn of a great awakening, a great remembering, something which has been in the making for a very long time. It is for you, of course, to think and decide for yourself.

Explore the traditions and directions that draw your interest. Trust your intuition. The most beautiful mystical realizations are both strangely bizarre and profoundly simple. It is often said that the ancient wisdom of magick takes only moments to teach, yet lifetimes to understand. This is the greatest quest there is.

Spell For Internal Well-Being

This simple spell has been very effective in harmonizing our inner mechanisms and bringing a feeling of well being and inner peace.

1. Obtain a vial (about half a cup) of water from a steadily flowing river and put aside.

2. Light two blue candles and place at the north and south points of a circle.

3. Light two white candles and place at the east and west points of the same circle.

4. Scatter freshly picked lavender and crushed leaves of an iceberg rose evenly around the perimeter of the circle and sit within it, facing the north point.

5. Cross the arms loosely over the chest and focus your awareness on the breath entering your body and slowly spreading through it.

6. Return your focus slowly to your environment and extinguish the candles using the river water, kneeling before each as you do so, in the order north west east south.

A Moonbeam Spell To Bring On Sleep

Take your pillow to a dry area beneath the moonbeams. Sprinkle a rosemary infusion around it. Work in a counterclockwise manner as you repeat, Away from me the thoughts of day, away from me my worried ways.

Then change your direction to clockwise, altering the incantation to: When Luna smiles through night's sky, so sleep will come to tired eyes. No more to wake, no more to roam, rest is welcome in my home.

Repeat this last phrase as you put your head on the pillow every night. This spell is good for banishing or easing insomnia and obtaining a peaceful rest. It's best to try this spell when the Moon is just rising in the sky, especially with the Moon in Gemini or Aquarius.

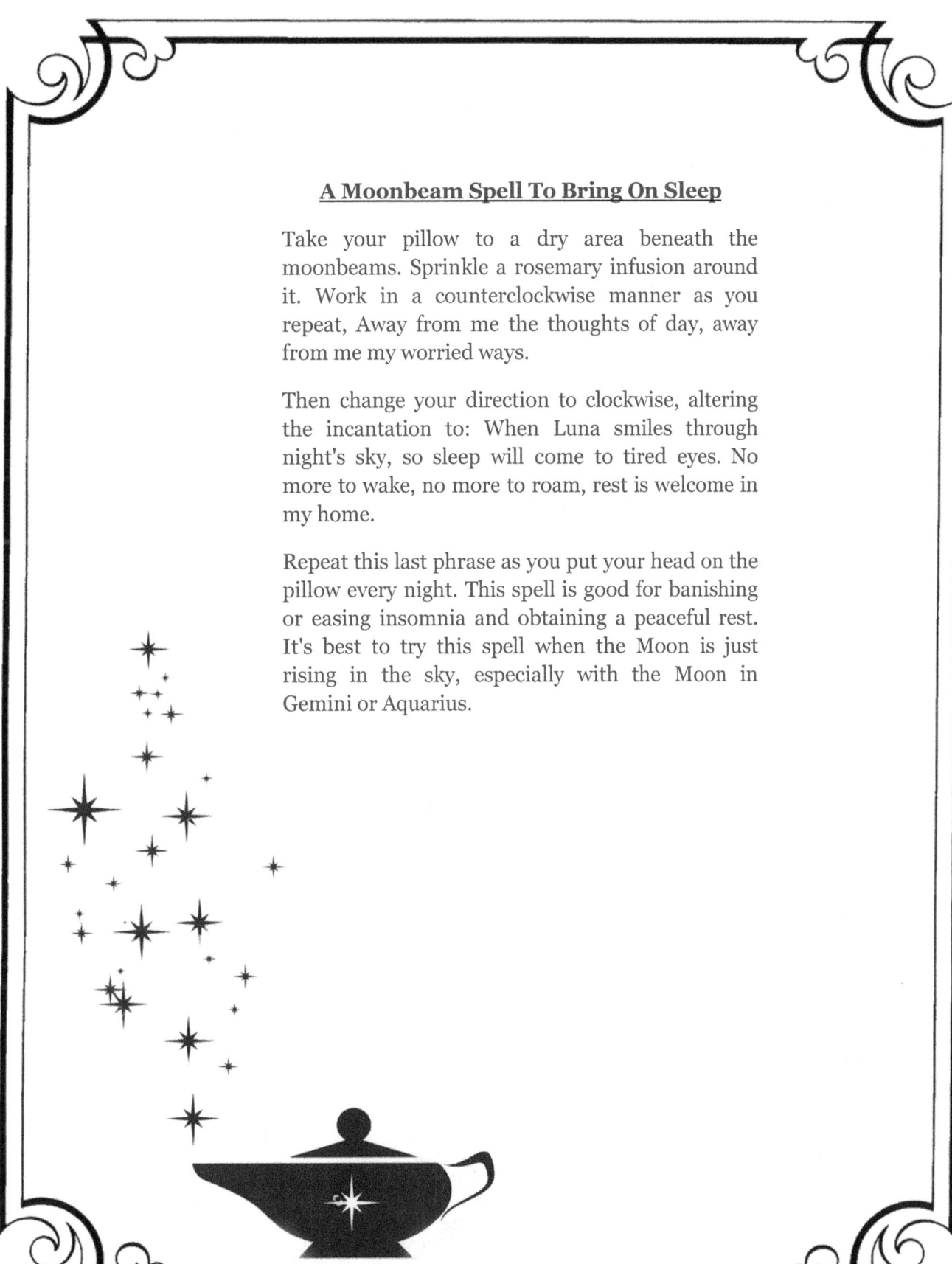

Spells For Protection

To protect an object, trace a pentagram over the object with your first and middle finger. Visualize that you're leaving a purple flame where you trace and say:

With this pentagram I lay Protection here both night and day And for he who should not touch Let his fingers burn and twitch I now invoke the rule of three So it shall be.

Here is a simple spell to protect an object. Again, trace a pentagram over the object that you wish to protect while saying:

With this pentagram Protection I lay To guard this object Both night and day And for him who should not touch May his body shiver and quake This I will So it will be.

Another spell for protection. Sit or stand before any fire. Look into the flames (or flame, if using a candle). Visualize the fire bathing you with glowing, protective light. The fire creates a flaming, shimmering sphere around you. If you wish, say the following or similar words:

Craft the spell in the fire, Craft it well, Weave it higher. Weave it now of shining flame, None shall come to hurt or maim. None shall pass this fiery wall, None shall pass, no, none at all.

Repeat this simple yet effective ritual everyday when in need.

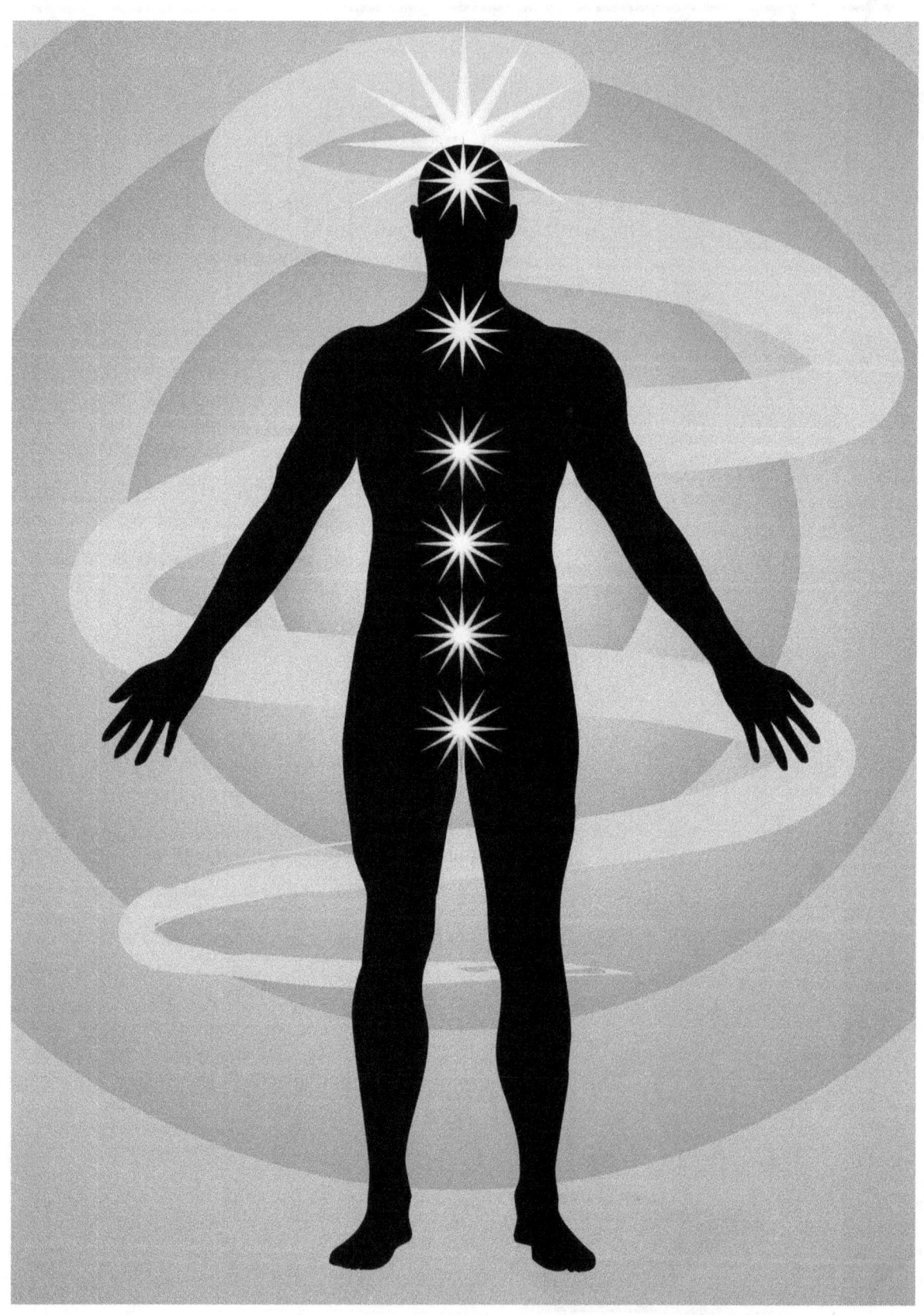

To Attract A Lover

This is when you have a lover but he or she is not as attentive as you wish they would be.

Sit before a dying fire and gaze into it, clearing your mind of all but thoughts of your lover.

Have a small basket of laurel leaves between your knees. Keeping your gaze fixed on the fire, dip your left hand into the basket, take out a handful of leaves, and toss them onto the fire.

As they burst into flames, chant out loud the following:

Laurel leaves that burn in the fire, Draw unto me my heart's desire.

Wait until the flames have died down, then repeat the action. Do it a third time. Within 24 hours your lover will come to visit you. If this spell doesn't work after a third time try this chant.

Lover come to me I hereby call, Do it before the new moon falls.

Gypsy-Witch Love Potion

(To be performed during the time of the waxing Moon on a Friday, on St. Agnes's Eve, or St. Valentine's Day, when the Moon is in Taurus or Libra).

Gather together a teaspoon of crushed dried basil, a teaspoon of dried fennel, a teaspoon of dried European vervain, three pinches of ground nutmeg and a quarter of a cup of red wine and cast a circle on the appropriate day.

Put the ingredients in a cauldron or pot and mix them up together. Heat the cauldron over a fire and light a pink candle anointed with rose oil. Concentrate on the object of your affection while brewing the potion and incant:

Candle light, warm and bright, Ignite the flames of love tonight. Let my soul mate's love Burn strong for me.

Boil the potion for three minutes before removing the cauldron from the fire to let it cool. Then strain it into a cup, add honey, and drink.

Or, you may drink half of the potion and let your beloved drink the other half.

Remember, using force will not work. A spell cast on a unwilling subject could bounce back at the spell-caster and cause bad luck and misfortune.

To Encourage Romance

Melt wax from a red candle and let it cool only until it is still malleable.

Place it in a bowl while you take three of the following herbs: Rose, dill, daisy, hibiscus, licorice, rosemary, basil, ginger, thyme, vanilla, geranium, juniper.

Mix the herbs, concentrating on your need for love. Knead the wax, adding a pinch of the herb mixture every few seconds until the wax is full of herbs.

Form the wax into a heart. Wrap it in pink cloth and hang it from your bed.

As well, you can make an herbal charm to attract love by filling a circle of rose or red colored cloth with any of the following: Acacia, rose, myrtle, jasmine, or lavender petals, in combination or singly.

Add to this a red felt heart and copper coin or ring.

As you fill the bundle with your chosen items, visualize the type of lover you are looking for.

Tie the cloth with blue thread or ribbon, in seven knots. As you tie the knots you may chant an incantation such as:

Seven knots I tie above, Seven knots for me and love.

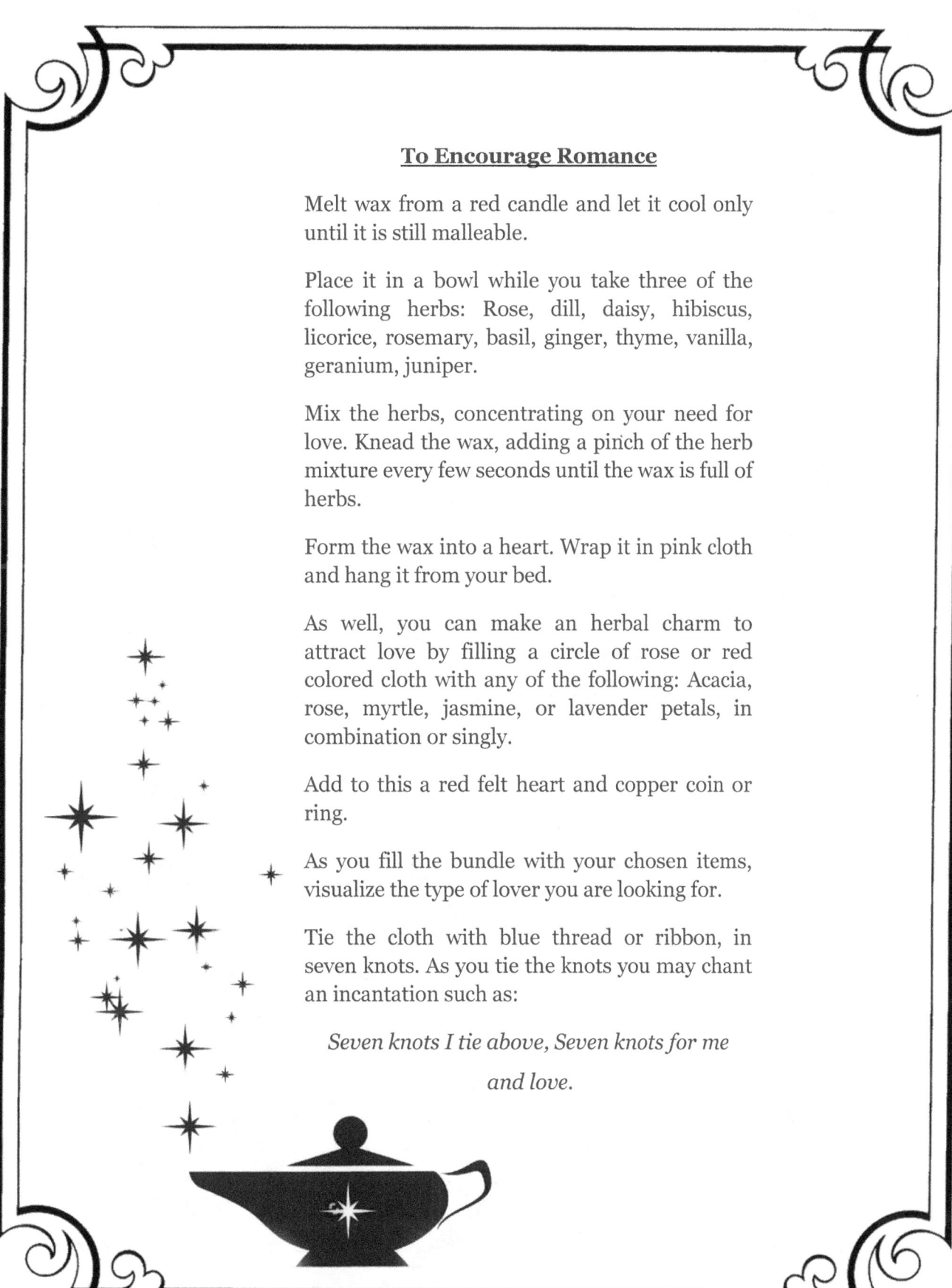

Are You Meant For Each Other?

If you are not sure whether you and your mate are meant for each other, and you are willing to forfeit the relationship should this not be the case, do this love spell.

Take two silver dollars. Two pennies will also do. Toss them into the air reciting:

May we each go to our own true love.

Do not do this spell unless you only want to be with a true love and so are willing to forfeit your present relationship should it not represent your true love.

Your true loves should reveal themselves within a month.

So, if you find that you are not meant for each other, this is an ideal spell for people who are bothered by a persistent suitor or stalker.

This spell should be done during the waning cycle of the Moon, that is, after the Full Moon and before the New Moon.

Have a roaring fire going, then go outside and pick up two handfuls of dry vervain leaves (you can place them on the ground ahead of time, if necessary.)

As you pick them up, shout out the name of the one you wish to be rid of. Turn and go into the house (or cross to the fire if this is all done out in the open) and fling leaves onto the fire with the words:

Here is my pain; Take it and soar. Depart from me now and offend me no more.

Do this for three nights. You will hear no more from your unwanted lover.

To Obtain Money

An extremely simple yet effective spell for obtaining fast money when needed is the following:

On a Friday during the Waxing Moon anoint a green candle with an appropriate money drawing oil, such as Patchouli, Jasmine, or Cinnamon.

Take the candle and place in a holder. Place a brand new shiny penny in front of the holder, and then surround the holder with three green aventurine gemstones.

Repeat the following chant 3 times:

Money, money come to me, $100 is what I need. With harm to none and help to many, multiply now this shiny penny!

Now light your candle and gaze into its flame, strongly visualizing the needed money coming to you.

Continue with this visualization for as long as possible.

After the candle has burned down completely, bury any remaining wax on your property and carry the penny with you to reinforce your magickal intention.

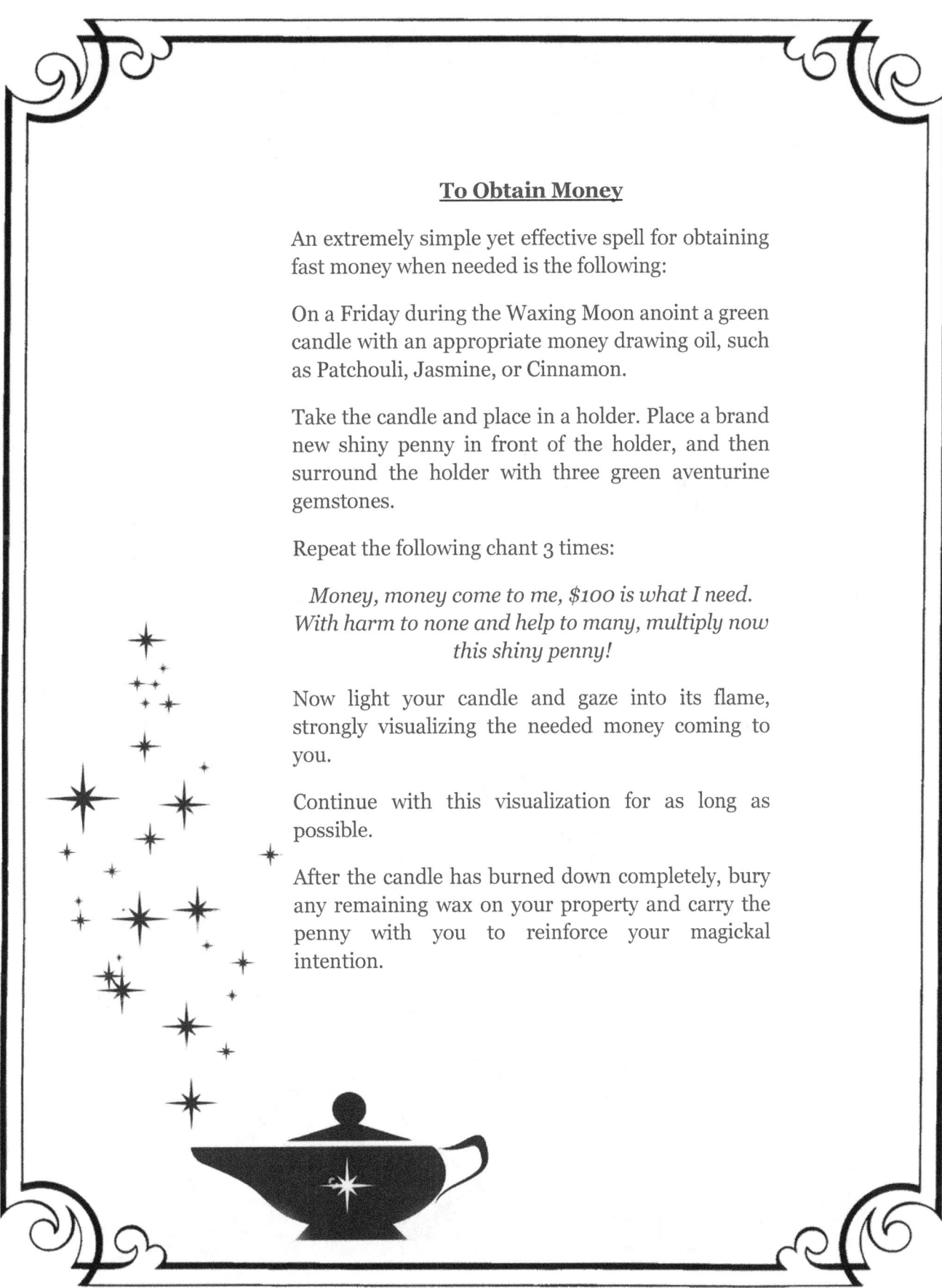

Simple Candle Spell To Bring Money

You will need one green candle, a candle holder. Do this visualization during the two weeks when the Moon is increasing in light, from New to Full.

Close your eyes and breathe slowly and deeply until you feel completely relaxed. Imagine yourself surrounded by a bright bubble of white light and protected from harm.

Begin to visualize money flowing into your life. You don't have to imagine how this is going to happen. In your mind's eye see dollar bills or silver dollars or whatever signifies money to you being blown towards you from above and from all directions. What does it feel like to have this money, to have the ability to pay all your bills or the freedom to buy what you most want? Try to both mentally picture this as clearly as you can and feel it emotionally.

Now pick up the candle and hold it tightly in your hands until you feel your pulse throbbing beneath your fingers. Your energy and the prosperous energies of the universe symbolized by the green candle are merging together. You are becoming a prosperity magnet. Affirm your desire (to yourself or out loud). For example:

Money streams continuously into my life, with harm towards none.

Continue visualizing and chanting as you place the candle in the holder and light it. Cup your hands around the flame, feeling its warmth and energy. Put the candle in a safe place and let it burn down naturally.

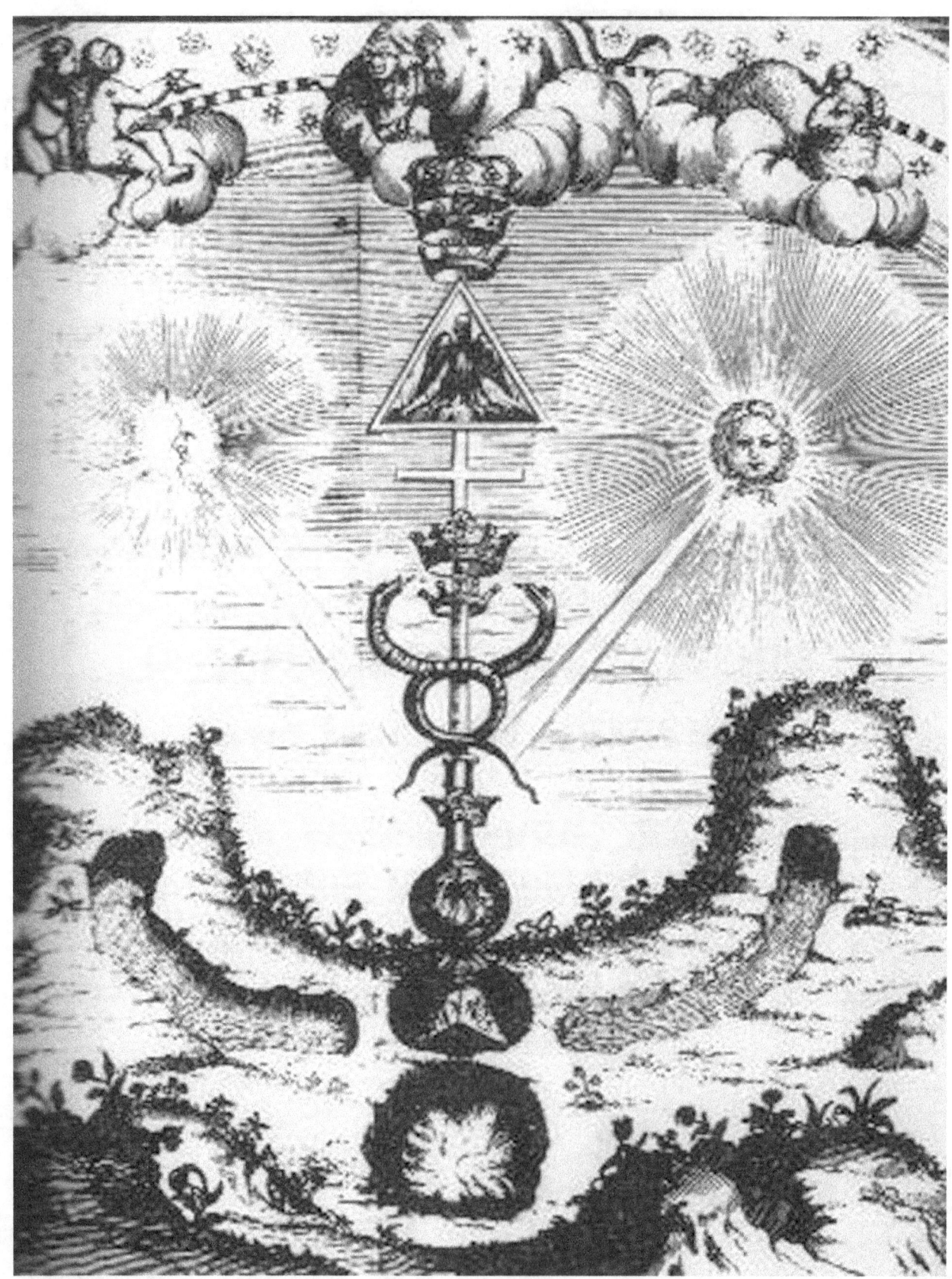

Business Success Oil

To make an anointing oil to bring business success, you will need:

6 drops Bergamot (Mint Bouquet) oil

2 drops Basil oil

2 drops Patchouli oil

1 pinch of ground Cinnamon (herb, not oil)

One half ounce base oil (apricot kernel, jojoba, grapeseed, even olive oil).

This is a very simple recipe, which has a multitude of uses, including: Anointing candles for business, prosperity rituals, anointing of hands, combine with bath salts for prosperity ritual baths, add to loose money drawing incense blends to increase its potency, anointing of talismans and charms, anoint the cash register, business cards, or the front door of a place of business to increase cash flow.

Keep in mind that for calling magick, such as money, love, health, or luck, it is best to perform the spells during the waxing moon (first quarter) to the full moon.

The universe works by taking the path of least resistance. That means the universe will place you into the nearest reality that conforms to your wishes.

You may not receive your desires exactly the way you wanted them. I have heard stories of people who used magick spells for money, only to have their house burn down. The money then came from the insurance settlement.

Throw Money To The Floor

The first part of this spell requires that you find some coins; you don't need a lot, just whatever you can find.

Next, scatter them on the floor of your house. You want to scatter them in a location where they can remain untouched and fairly out in the open for seven days.

As you scatter the coins, say out loud:

Money on the floor brings money in the door.

Once a day, return to the coins and repeat the chant.

Money on the floor brings money in the door.

At the end of seven days, gather the coins and keep them together for seven more days.

At the end of those seven days, spend the coins knowing that they have accomplished their task.

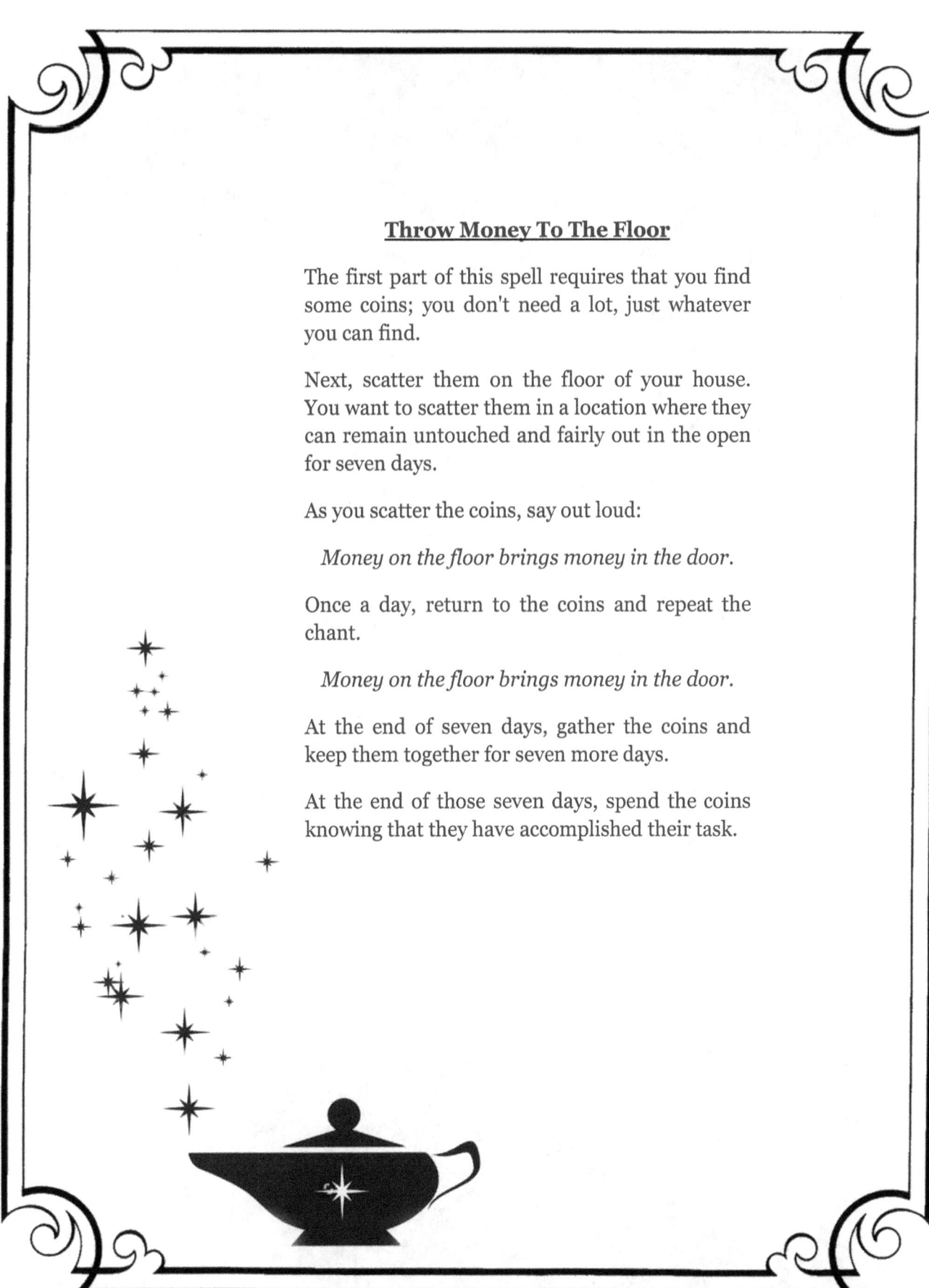

Banish Fear

This is a powerful spell used to prevent the spirits of fear from bringing suffering into one's life.

At the rising of the sun, on the twelfth day of the month, a piece of clean, white, fine cloth should be laid flat upon a table. An equal mixture of thyme, rosemary and freshly ground ginger root should be spread over it, evenly distributed, but not too heavy.

The following invocation need be spoken aloud:

Spirit of the Rising Sun Enter this place

Allow thy face to shine brightly upon this offering

That thy grace may be invoked.

The Spirit of Fear hath taken up residence in mine humble home and apprehension has settled in not to be easily shaken loose

Spirit of the Rising Sun hear my plea Let these spirits no more bother me

Banish them to darkness and bid them take leave.

Spirit of the Rising Sun fill the empty corners That lo, they may not loiter and hide

Sweep the rooms with thine mighty hand Force them outside.

Spirit of the Rising Sun I invoke your power that these things for which I ask Be done

So it was, so it is, so it shall ever be.

Gather the cloth and take it outside and shake it completely clean and then washed using soap and hot water.

Sleep Well and Have Sweet Dreams

To help you sleep peacefully and have pleasant dreams, create a tranquil and calming environment for your bedroom.

The windows should have either curtains or walls that are light coloured or pastel tones and make sure the bed head is well away from the door.

Cleanse the atmosphere of your room by holding a sprig of lavender and walking through the room with a peaceful mind and heart.

At bedtime turn off everything in the room that could be distracting or disturbing, like television and loud music or radios.

Put a lavender sachet under your pillow and before go to sleep say to yourself,

Feather light on starry night,

cosy warm and tired,

pleasant dreams and sweetest thoughts

as little angels smile.

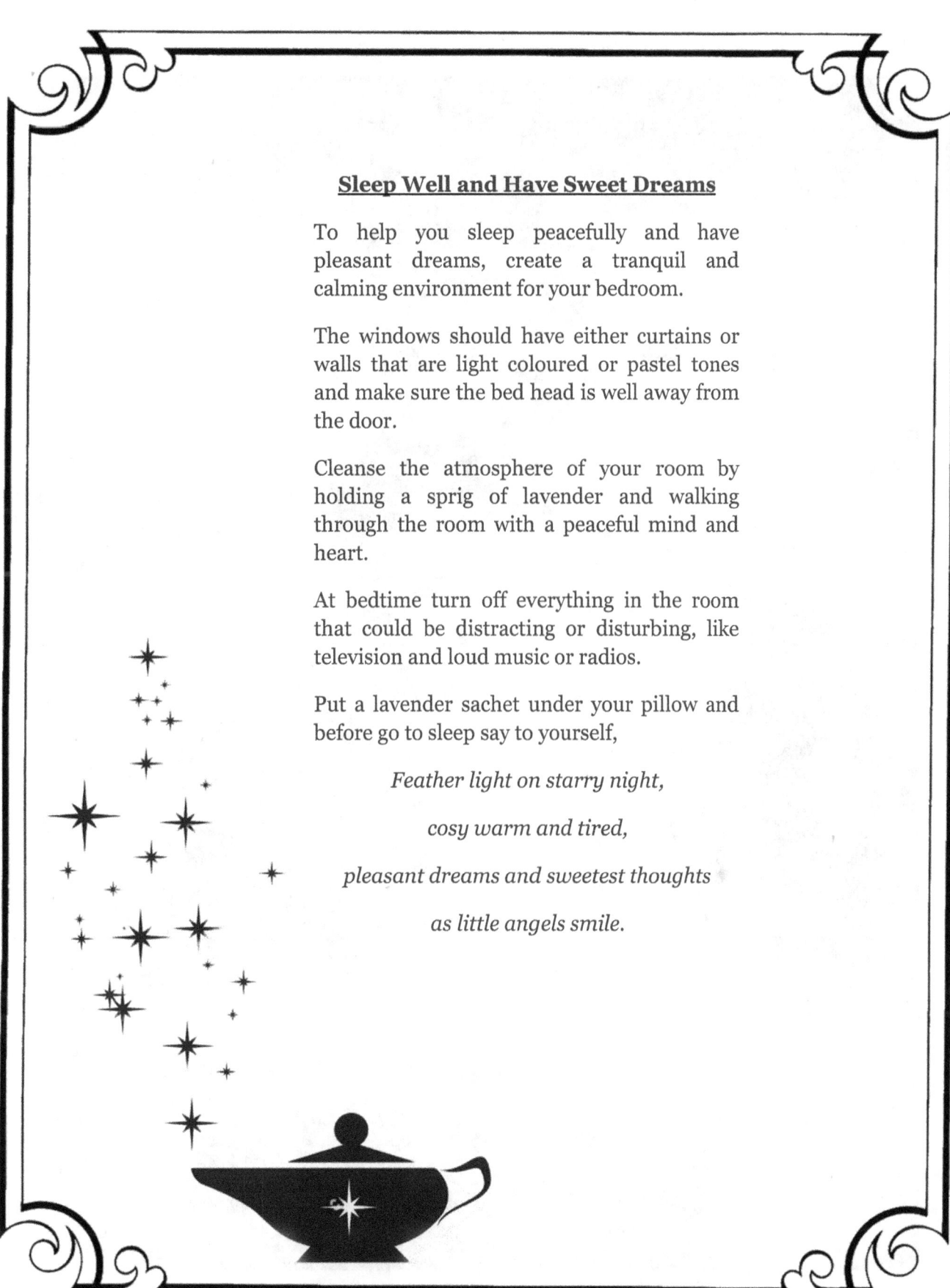

Spell to Draw Positive Energy

This spell will draw anything that gives positive energy, be it friends, good luck or general happiness. The items you will need are:

A small magnet

1 candle

A flame-proof dish

A small piece of paper and pen

Sit down and light a candle in front of you. Focus all your thoughts on becoming positive. Take a deep breath and write down on a piece of paper anything that you want.

Wrap this paper around the magnet and squeeze it, visualizing that you are inducing positive energy into it. At the same time chant the following verses:

This magnet will attract and draw good energy to me. Good things will come my way and I'll accept them happily.

Unwrap the paper and set it on fire. Quickly throw it in the fireproof dish and imagine that all the energy you put in the paper is being released into the universe.

Allow the candle to burn out and carry the magnet with you so the positive energies can be drawn to you.

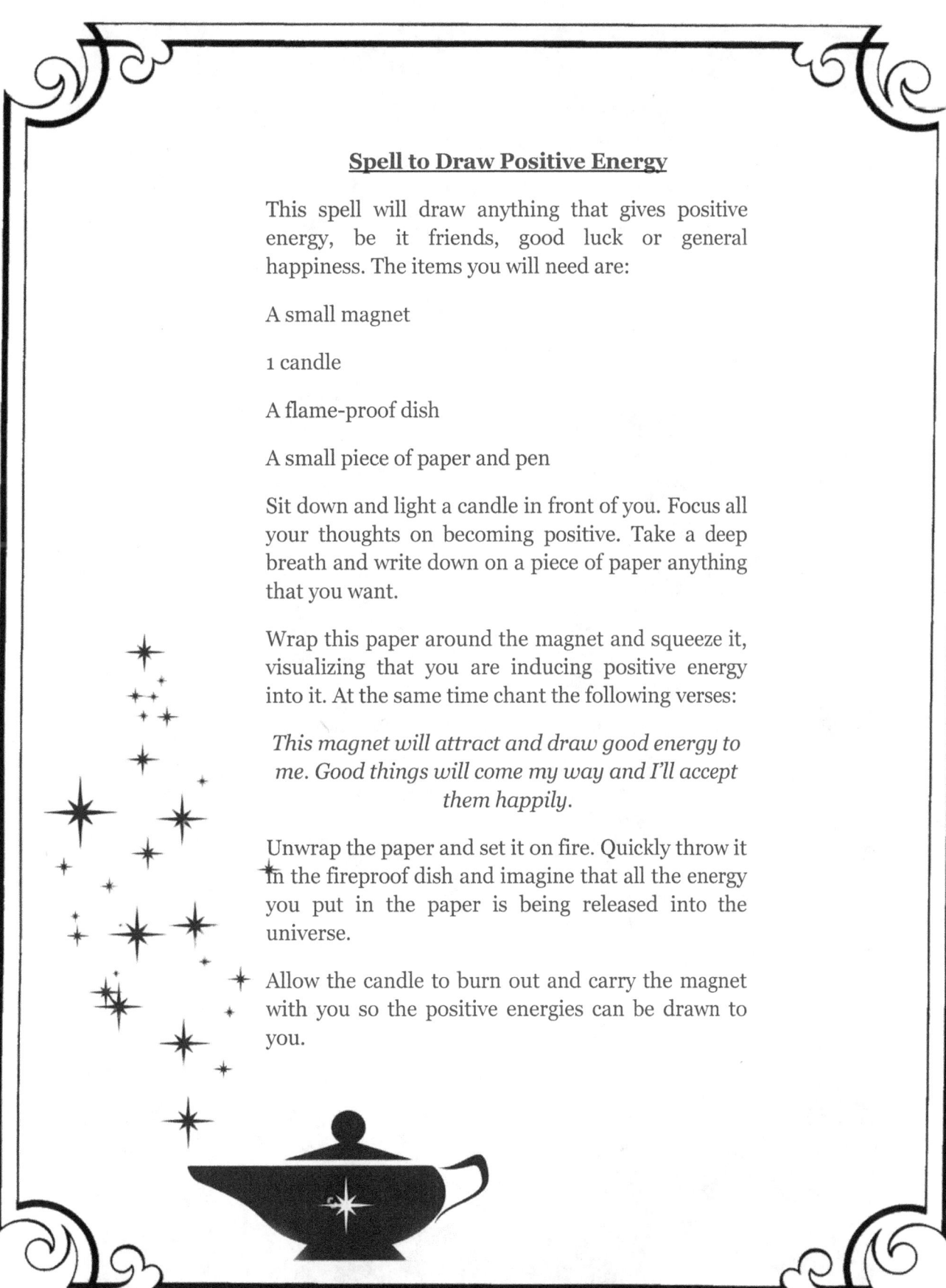

Summon Beauty From Within

Stand in front of a mirror, closing your eyes as you do so. It is suggested to do this daily.

Say the following spell:

Beauty energy within me,

Grow your roots from my heart to my body.

-Imagine beautiful, glamourous, extraordinary energy being delivered from your beautiful heart to your physical body, or a part (Face, skin, hands, etc.) Feel and see it replenish your beauty, increasing your charismatic appearance. And always remember; beauty is from within, and every human is beautiful in their own way.

Next say:

I am beautiful, from the inside....out.

Repeat this spell once a day for seven days.

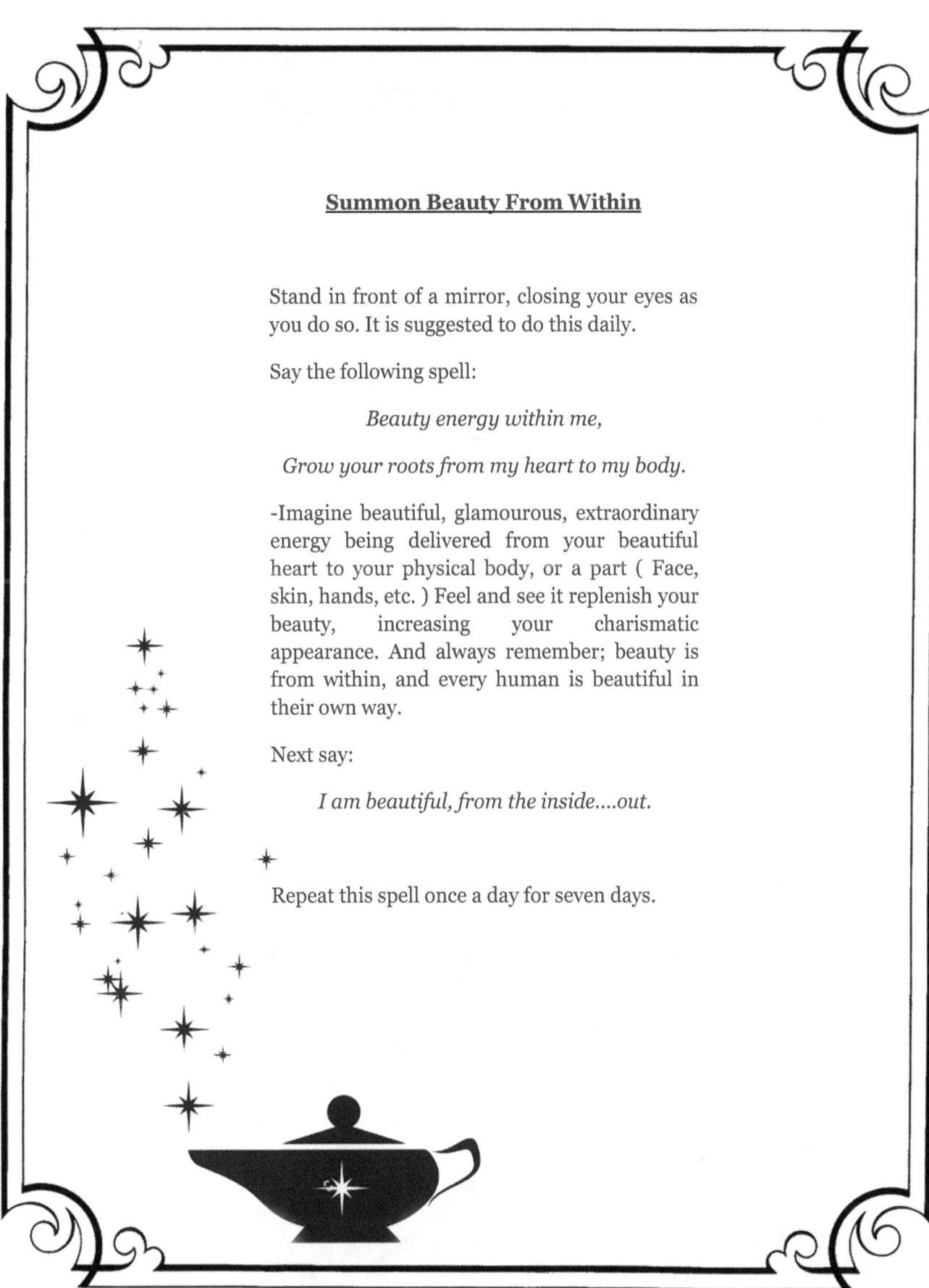

Make Your Wish A Reality

Tear out a piece of paper that is about an inch or two in length and width.

It's best to use a pen, or maker, and not a pencil.

Write down the following:

Your name

Your birthday

Your wish

Current date

Chant the following:

> *While many without faith may dismiss,*
>
> *I promise to always believe in this wish,*
>
> *and in the things I am let to learn,*
>
> *so grant me this wish I soulfully yearn.*

While still chanting the following, fold the paper three times and place it in the candle.

Watch the paper burn and continue to chant.

Imagine the outcome. When you think the wish will come true, you can either let the paper burn out, or blow the candle out.

Depending on the wish, this spell usually works by the following day.

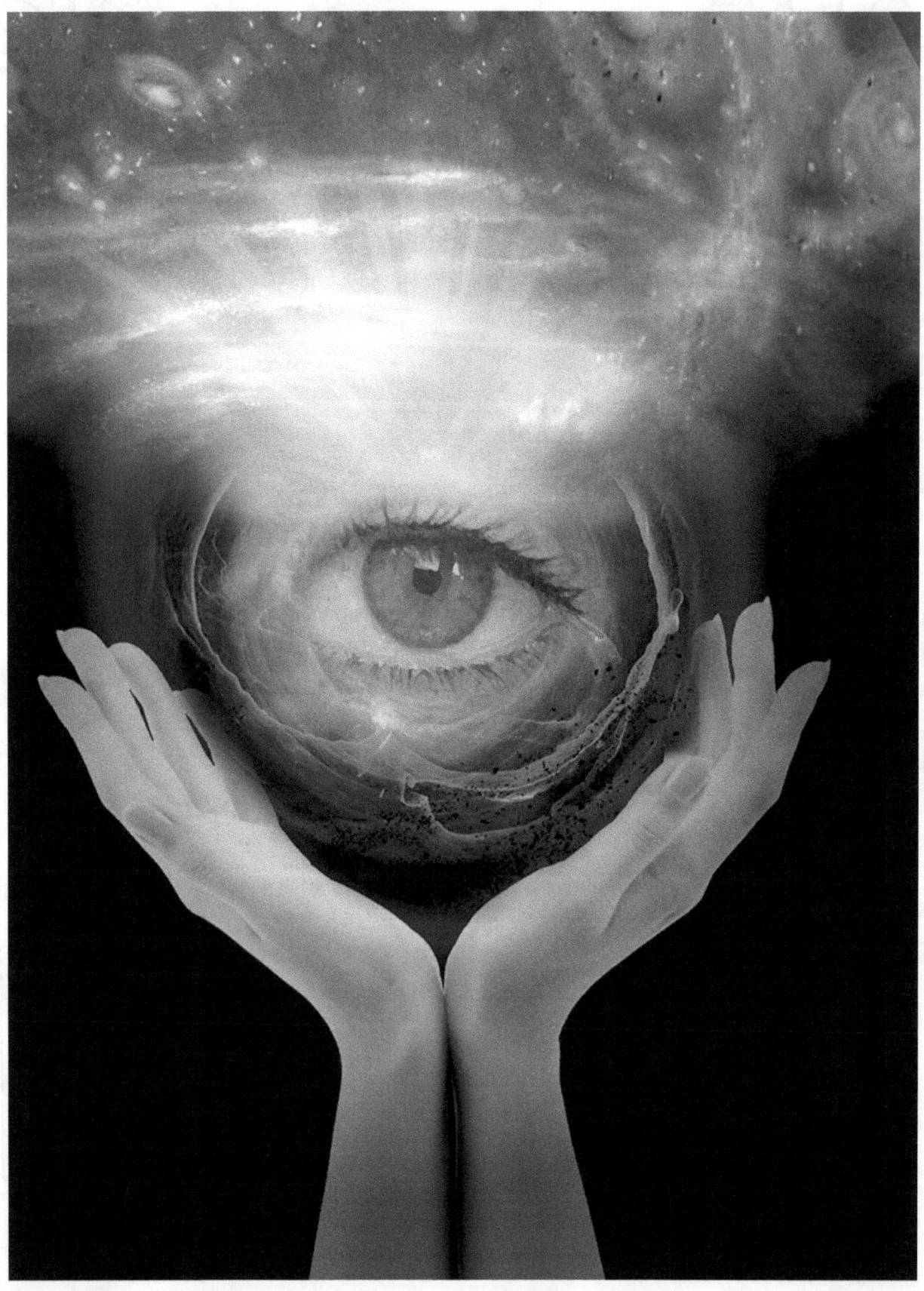

Call Forth The Power of The Universe

In a quiet place, close your eyes and imagine the area just above your abs and below your heart...the solar plexus. Envision a bright, glowing ball of light. The ball grows larger until it fills your belly, and traveling to your sacral and base chakras that are below the belly button.

Now, imagine the ball of light shooting into your central nervous system like bolts of lightning.

With eyes closed, say firmly but in a low tone:

Powers of the universe within me rise. Rise, rise rise like the incoming tide, tide tide. In and out and in you flow, from my head and down to my toes. Inward and outward and inward you go, flowing freely, go go go! Powers of the universe within me rise, rise rise rise with might...this is my will.

Repeat chant until it is said three times. It will focus your entire being on magic and your abilities.

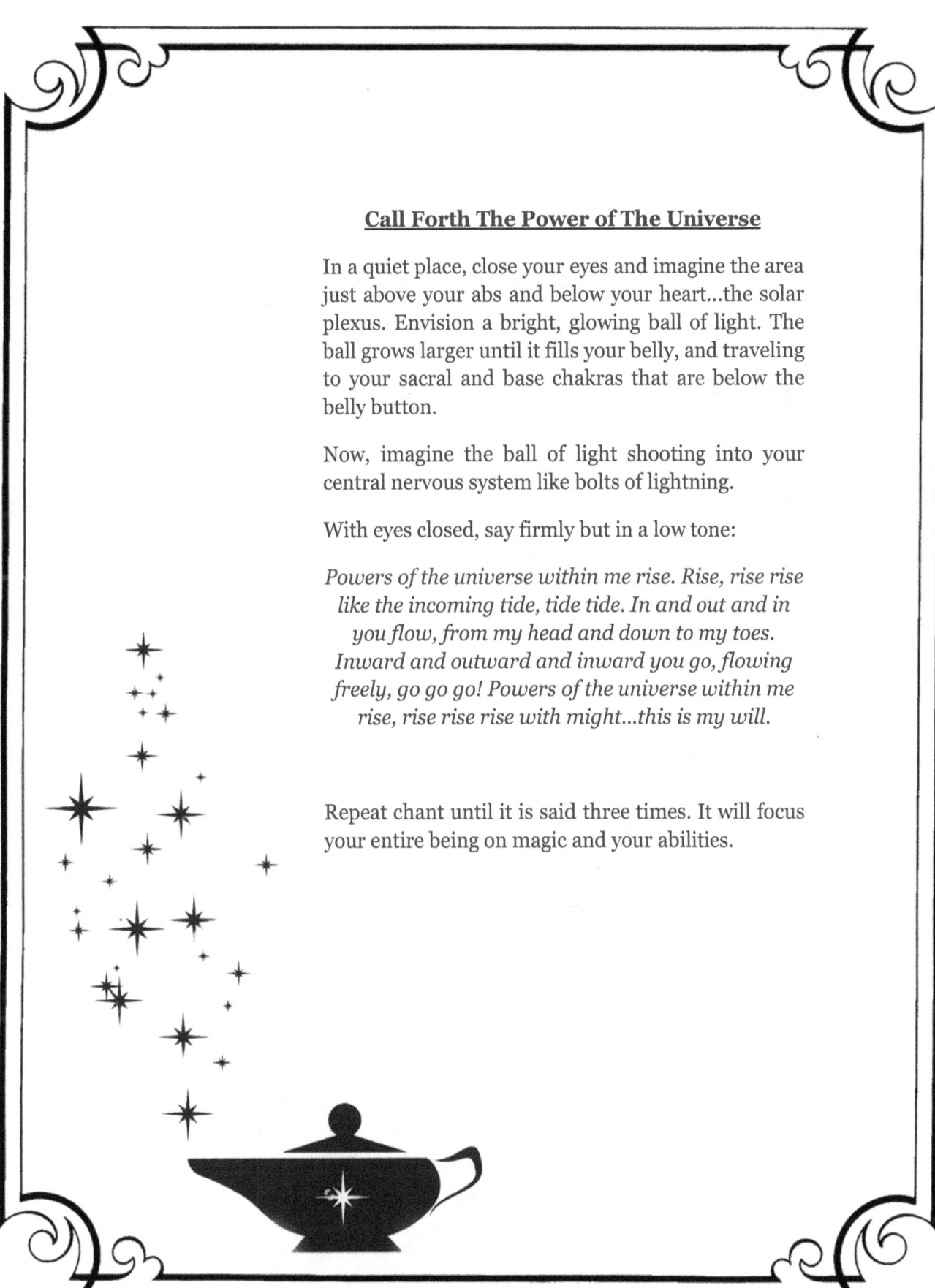

Personal Magick Charm

This spell is to create a personal magick charm. This charm will assist you in keeping bad luck away and drawing good luck. As well, it will enpower your wishes and help provide energy for any magick spells that you do.

You will need the following items for this spell:

1 Blue candle

1 Red candle

1 Purple candle

1 Green Candle

1 Black cadle

1 Yellow candle

A lighter or match

1 item you wish to create a charm out of (examples: coin, crystal, pendant, braclet etc.)

Line up the candles in this order in front of you from the right to left: Red, Black, Green, Blue, Purple and Yellow. Then light them in order from left to right. Hold the item you have chosen to be your charm in both hands up over the top of your head. Speak the following clearly and strongly...

Love, Death, Enrichment, Spirit, Protection and Life. These I so call upon to have and to share my own experienced knowledge and I wish for you to take from me what I desire of you.

Extinguish the candles as you lit them. Keep your charm with you at all times for it now holds a part of your own power.

Make Bad Luck Go Away

In the night, light a fire in a firepit or campfire. You can also do this spell inside using a fireplace.

Write on a piece of paper the words BAD LUCK. Then write down any bad things you do not like in your life right now. Next, draw a big X across the paper with a black marker. While doing this you should be thinking of how all these things are going to disappear from your life, never to return. Place the paper in the fire and repeat the following words 3 times:

Fire, fire burning bright

turn my darkness into light!

Take away my bad luck ill,

bring me nothing but goodwill.

Bad luck came and stayed to long,

be gone forever, be gone, be gone!

With this fire burning bright,

bring me good luck, bring me light!

After repeating these words 3 times, sit for a few minutes and concentrate on the bad luck being gone and the good luck coming your way! Allow the fire to burn out on its own.

House Protection Spell

You will need the following items for this spell:

Salt

House Blessing Incense

Holders

Step1: light your house blessing incense and place them in the holders. Place them where they won't be bothered by anybody.

Step2: Place them in each room of the house, and make sure the incense is lit as you set them in each room of the house.

Step3: Sprinkle a little salt in each room, and then say these words:

Lord and Lady, I ask thee to protect this house from evil that may bring harm to this house, and also protect those inside and outside this house so no harm will come to them.

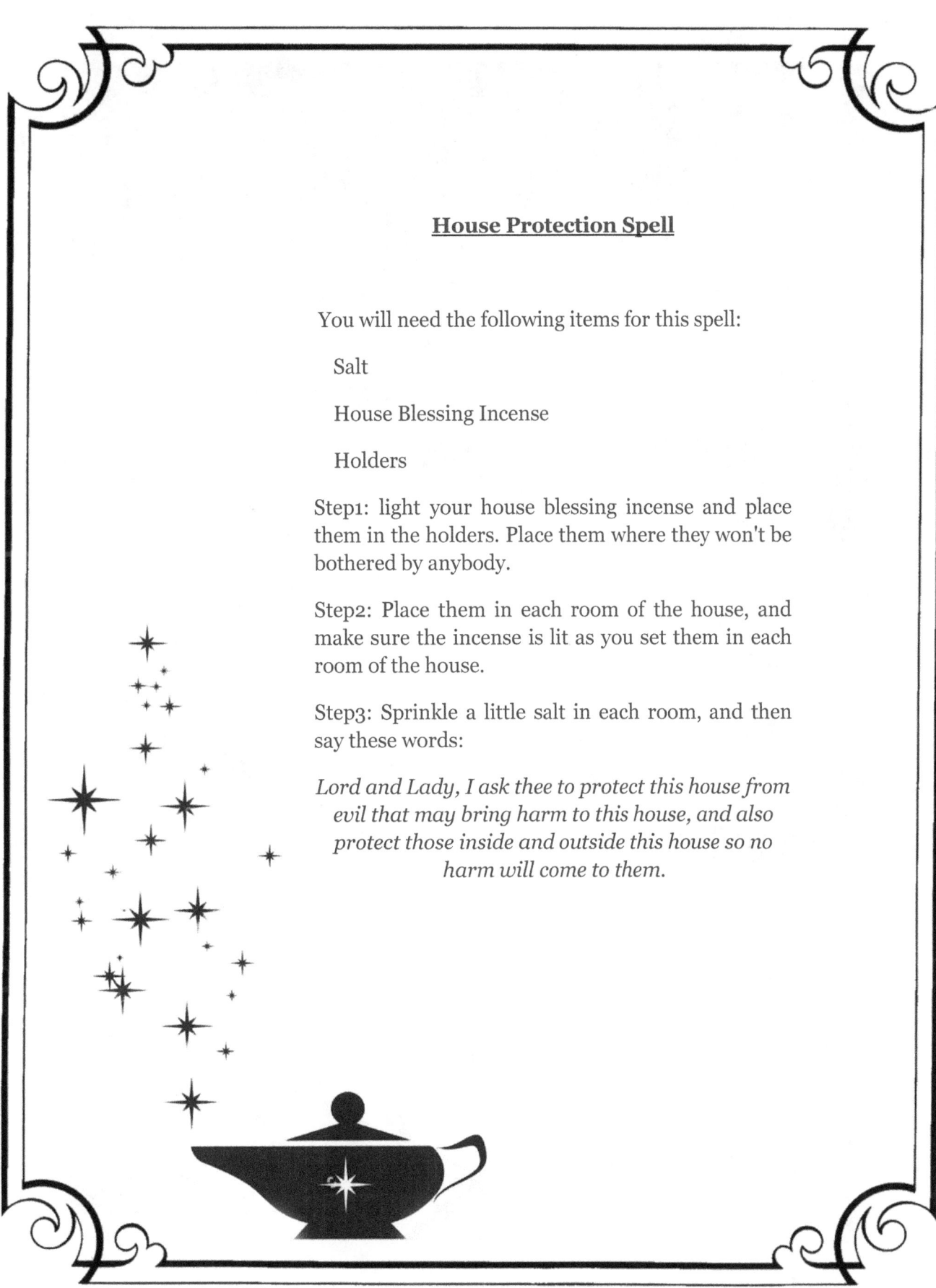

Love, Healing, and Protection Satchet

You will need the following items for this spell:

2 Cinnamon Sticks or Cinnamon Powder

Chamomile

Spearmint

Yarrow Flower

Cloves

A satchet

Putting your intention in, you will want to mix all herbs together in a satchet. The color can be any, but should be colors like Pink, White, or Green.

When done correctly, this bag will draw in the energies of Love, Healing and Protection. Keep your satchet with you at all tmes.

Be sure to have properly grounded yourself as too much energy will make your body become unbalanced.

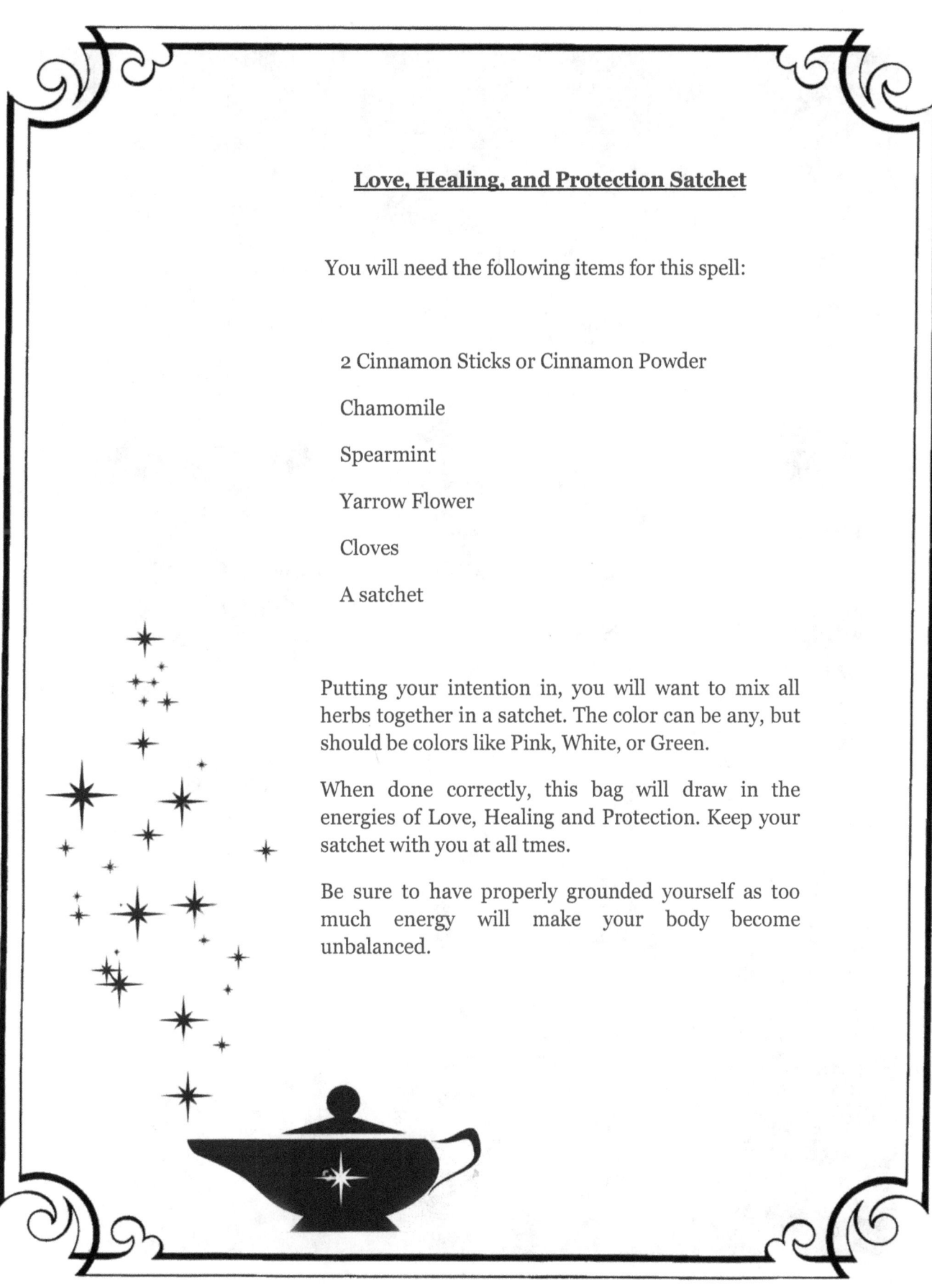

Healing Candle Spell

You will need the following items for this spell:

3 light blue candles

A knife or something you can use to carve your candles

Candle Holders

Carve your name (or the person's name) into the wax of all three candles. Set them into the holders and light them. Then Repeat the following:

Healing light,

shining tonight.

The power i feel,

be used to heal.

Now concentrate on the illness or condition that you are looking to heal. Let the candles burn out when you are finished.

Gain The Favor of The Moon

This spell is used for gaining the favor of the powers of the Moon. It is an excellent spell for adding vitality to your life.

You will need the following items for this spell:

Moon Oil or natural vegetable oil

A small glass of your favorite beverage

On the eve of a full moon, close to midnight, dip the tip of your right index finger into either Moon Oil or natural vegetable oil and trace a pentacle on a flat surface, such as a tabletop or counter top. Light five candles and place one at each point of the pentacle. In the center of the pentacle, place a small glass of your favorite beverage.

Recite the following incantation:

I call to the Moon that her powers cast upon this night

Be caught and kept, consumed in faith

Revered and praised, used for the good intent

That no evil shall pass, lest all be undone

And this spell be for naught

Bright moon, may your blessings and energy

Live within me

Quickly, drink the beverage and starting at any point, extinguish the candles in a clockwise rotation.

Make Any Item A Good Luck Charm

This spell will make any item a portable good luck charm. Choose something small and easy to carry with you. You will need the following items for this spell:

Paper

Pen or Marker with green ink

The item you wish to charm

Any color yarn

Focus

This spell has to be performed at night or dawn. First you draw a pentagram on the piece of paper. Put the item you wish to charm in the center of the pentagram. Focus on the object and then imagine power flowing from your soul to the item.

Now say the following words:

> *Lady of luck please send some luck,*
>
> *make this item filled with luck, please*
>
> *send a lot, for it would be nice to not have*
>
> *bad luck. LUCK LUCK LUCK!*

After you chanted those words wrap your item in the yarn. You can then put your charm into a bag, make a necklace, whatever your creativity tells you to do. The key is that you want to keep your good luck charm with you.

Finally, soak the pentagram in water and then tear it up. After that the luck will be sealed into your charm.

Rose Love Spell

You will need the following items for this spell:

Red and purple paper

Rose oil

A picture of you and loved one

Scissors

A red pen

This charm requires all three traditional Charms: Verbal, Physical and written. Dab your paper with your rose oil while saying:

Rose of love, this charms begun,

That I and (name of person)

Will always be one!

Cut the paper in a shape of a heart.

In the middle of the picture put the picture of you and your love writing you names underneath and keep it in a safe place to safeguard that relationship and keep love alive.

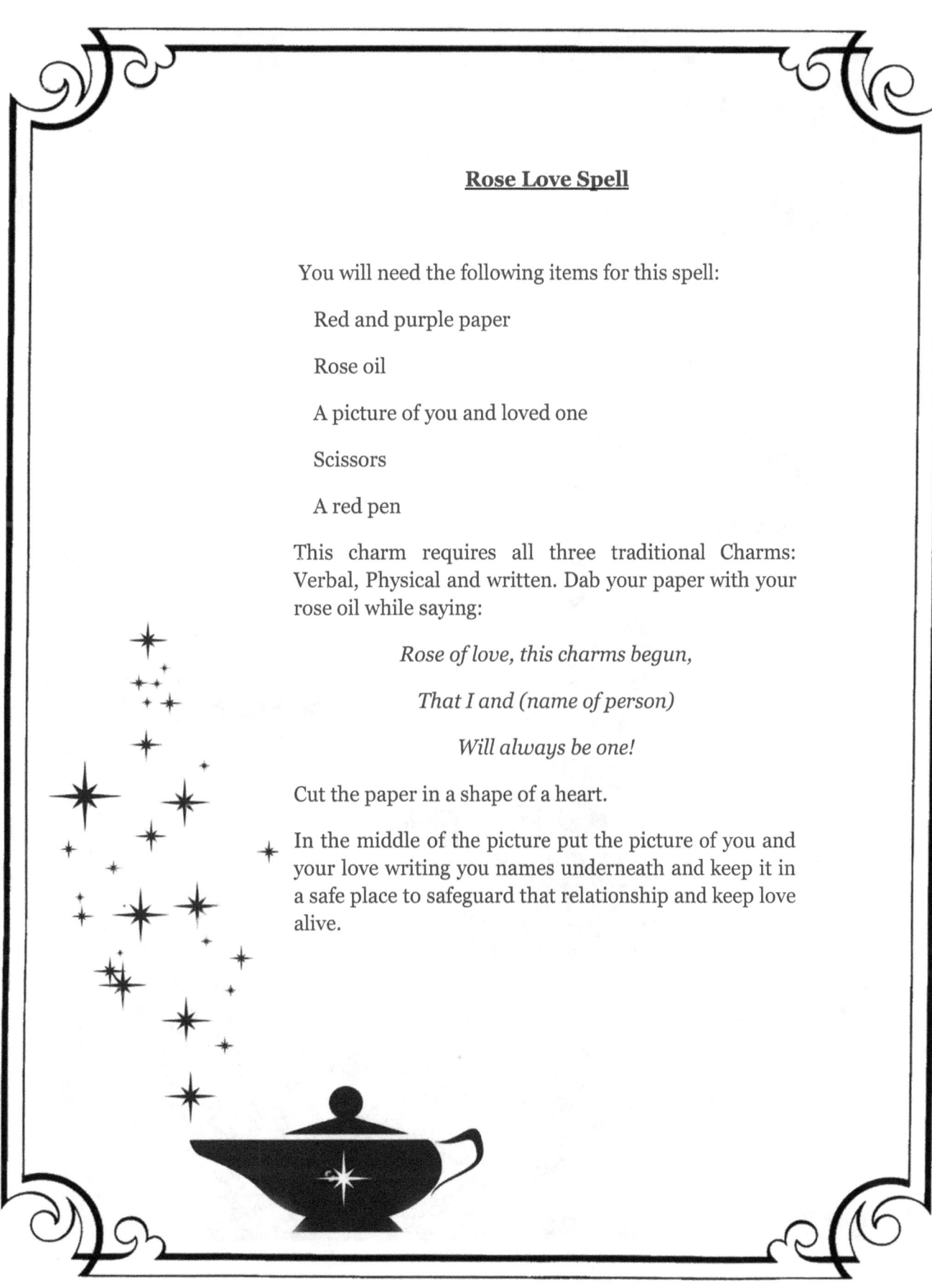

To Find The Truth

Without the truth one cannot make sensible decisions. As one's intuition grows it becomes easier to tell when people are not telling you the truth. Until that time a simple spell like this ensures that the truth is revealed in the right way. It uses herbs and candles.

You will need the following items for this spell:

Handful of thyme

Red candle

Flat dish or pentacle on which to put the herbs

Place the thyme into the dish and say:

Clarification I now require So that truth is spoken Let what is hidden now Be brought into the open.

Light the candle and say:

Speak truth with passion And goodbye to caution As the truth is said May I not be misled.

Allow the candle to burn down until the wax drips onto the herbs.

Bury the cooled wax and herbs, preferably at a crossroads, having first blown any loose herbs to the wind.

The herb thyme is said to bring courage, which is often needed to bypass our inhibitions. The color red often represents sexual passion, but here is much more the passion for truth. Remember therefore that sometimes the truth can hurt, and you may have been being protected.

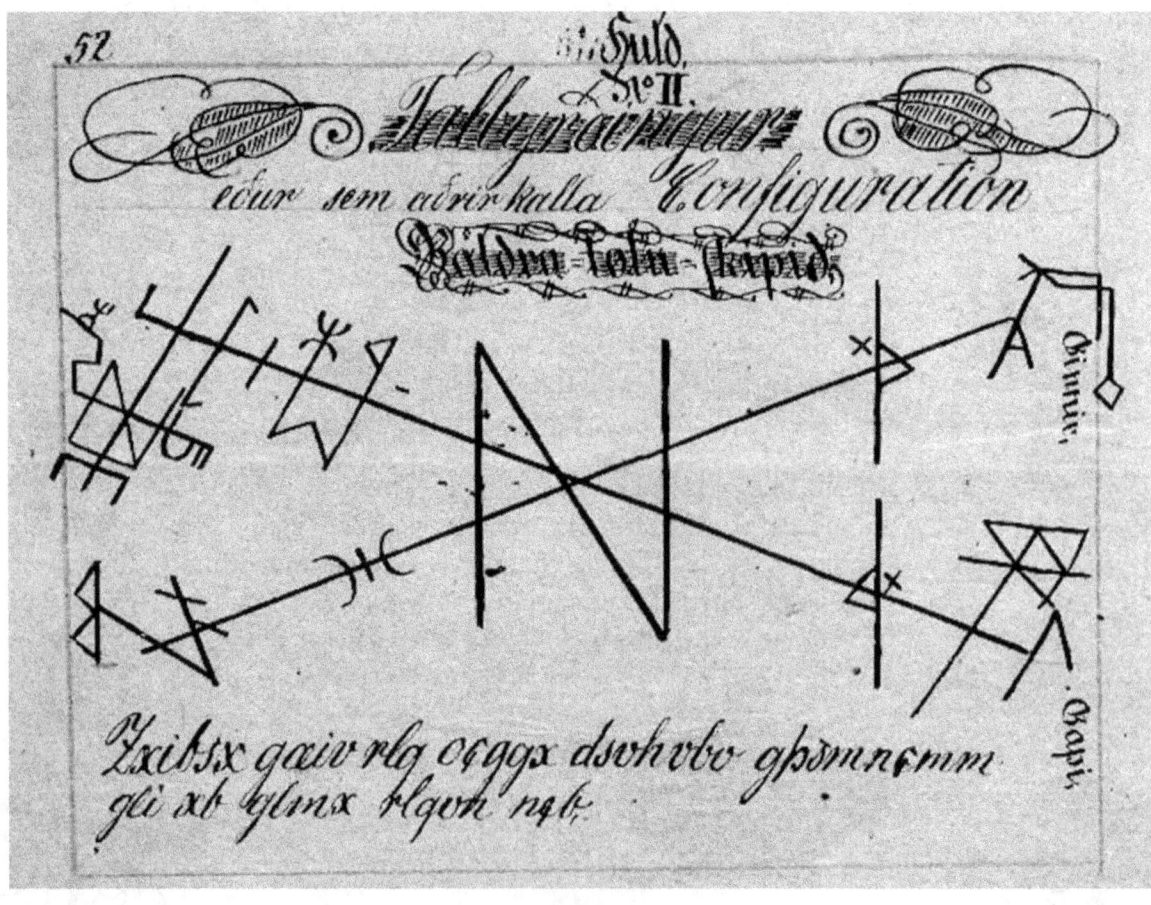

Powerful Love Spell

In this spell two ingredients are brought together to help you to enchant your loved one. Strawberries are well known as lovers' fruits.

Be aware that it is not right to influence the other person against their will or their natural inclinations. You should use this spell to prepare the ground for true relationship.

You will need the following items for this spell:

   Strawberry incense

   Pink candles

   A plate of strawberries

   Melted chocolate

Light the candles and the incense. Dip each strawberry in the chocolate. As you do so, visualize you and the other person together enjoying one another's company, becoming closer and so on. Say these words as you prepare the fruit:

> *Lover, lover, come to me*
>
> *And even then you shall be free*
>
> *To come, to go just as you please*
>
> *Until to stay your heart decrees.*

Serve the strawberries to your intended and enjoy the fruit together.

This spell can be quite powerful, particularly if you use the same pink candles when your lover arrives.

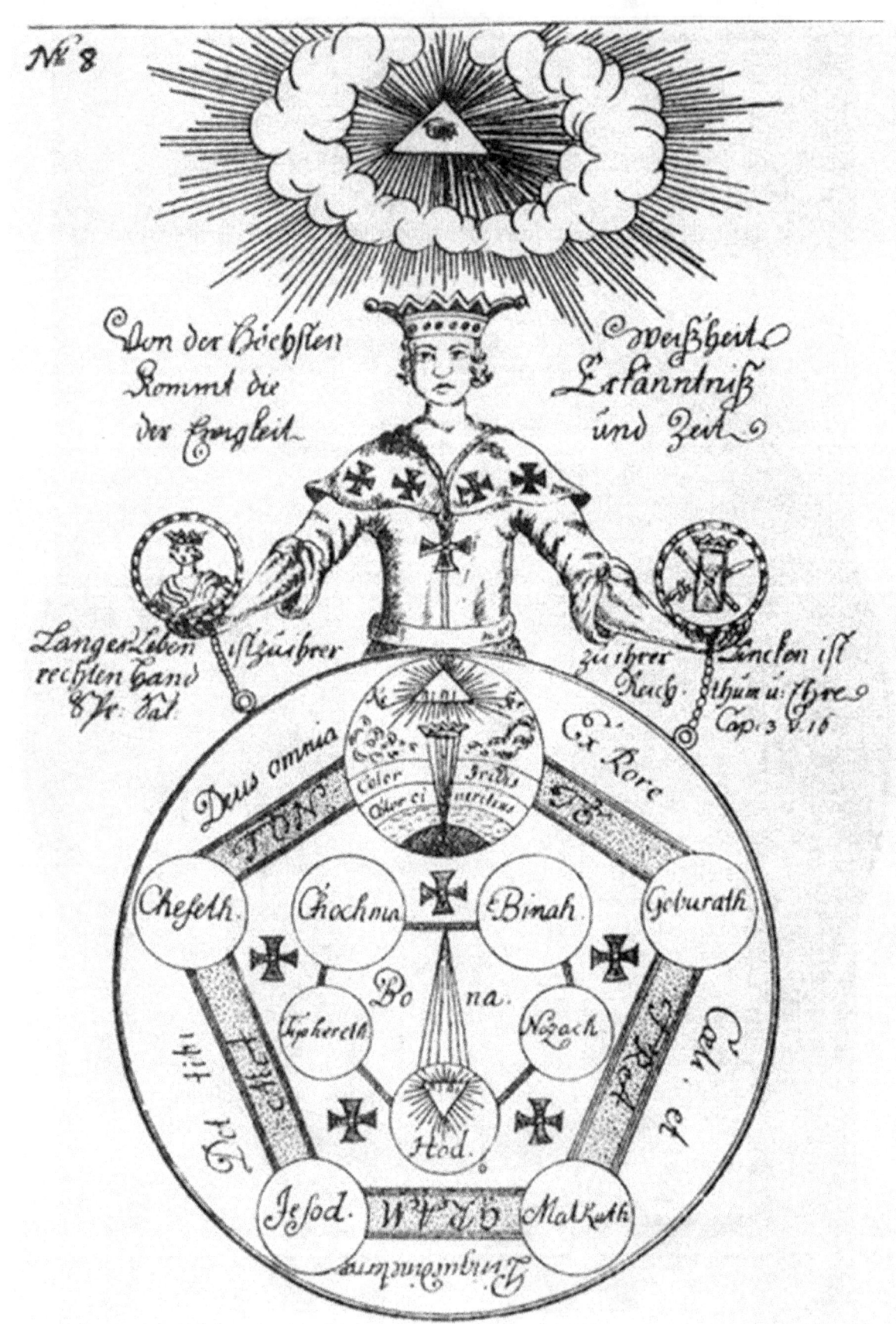

Attracting A New Friend

This spell draws to you a friend rather than a lover – someone of like mind who enjoys the same things that you do. It is best performed during the waxing phase of the Moon.

You will need the following items for this spell:

3 Brown Candles

Sheet of Paper

Pen

Light the candles and on the sheet of paper write down the attributes you would like your friend to have. Say each attribute out loud. Fold the paper in half twice. Light the edge of the folded paper from one of the candles and say these words:

With heart and mind I do now speak, Bring to me the one I seek, Let this paper be the guide and bring this friend to my side. Pain and loneliness be no more draw a companion to my door. Let not this simple spell coerce Or make my situation worse. As I will, it shall be.

Let the paper burn out then snuff out the candles. Use these candles only for the same type of spell.

Within the next few weeks, you should meet someone with some or all of the qualities you seek. Remember that you have called this person to you, so you can have the confidence and the time to explore the relationship properly. Never ever be judgmental about qualities in your new friend that are not ones that you have requested.

Candle Money Spell

An effective candle spell for wealth and prosperity utilizes two black candles since black draws in all color and energy in the universe.

Etch your name and the words "money", "wealth", "riches" and any other words of power along the sides of the candles. Then light the candles and grasp them firmly in your hands until you feel your pulse throbbing beneath your fingers, a sign that your aura is mingling with the candles' auras and that your intentions are firmly grounded in the candles.

Visualize what you want while saying:

These candles bring me wealth and riches.

In no way will this spell cause me to suffer any

adverse effects!

When finished extinguish the flame with a spoon, candle snuffer, or your fingers (not your breath, which will change the spell).

Begin this spell on Sunday, Thursday, or Friday as these days honor the sun, Jupiter, and Venus respectively.

Re-light the candles every night until they are completely burned down. Daily repetition will increase the spell's effectiveness and your own prosperity consciousness.

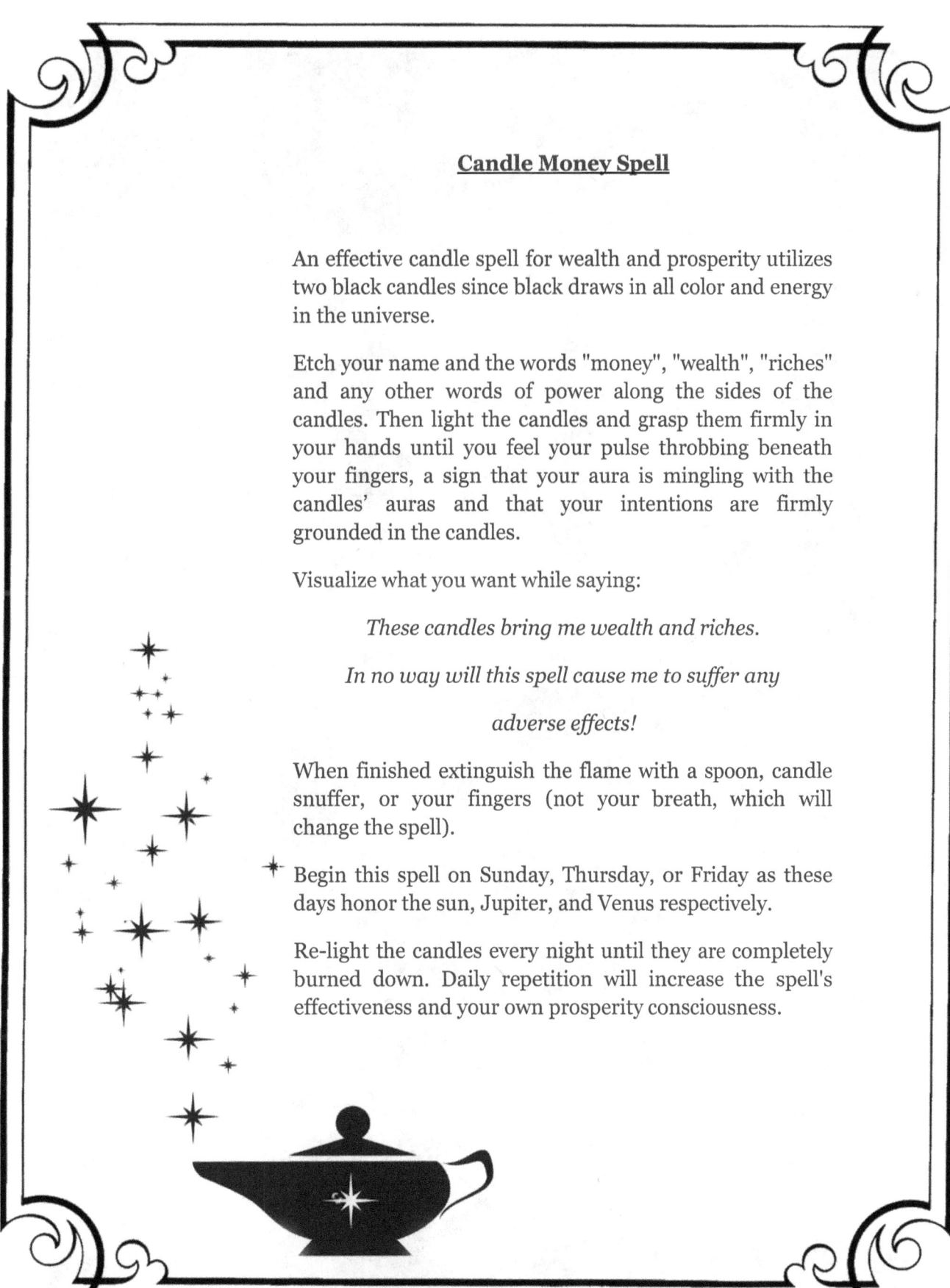

Solve Cash Flow Problem

Can be used if money is irregular, or to be repaid money owed.

You will need the following items for this spell:

- Brown candle (prosperity)
- An orange (money, happiness)
- Paper and pen
- Cinnamon
- Dried orange peel,
- Basil,
- Patchouli,
- Vervain (all money and active-oriented herbs)
- A dollar coin

On the slip of paper, write **"money come, money flow, money dance, money grow"**. Wrap the dollar coin in the paper. Blend the herbs; sprinkle a pinch into the paper packet. Make a slice about halfway into the orange; insert the paper-wrapped coin. Burn remaining herbs on charcoal while holding the orange and chanting the same chant you wrote on the paper. Keep the orange on the altar for seven days.

Ideally, this spell should be done between first quarter to full moon. On the day of the full moon, remove the dollar and spend it, preferably in aid of some charity cause. Money needs to move to flow.

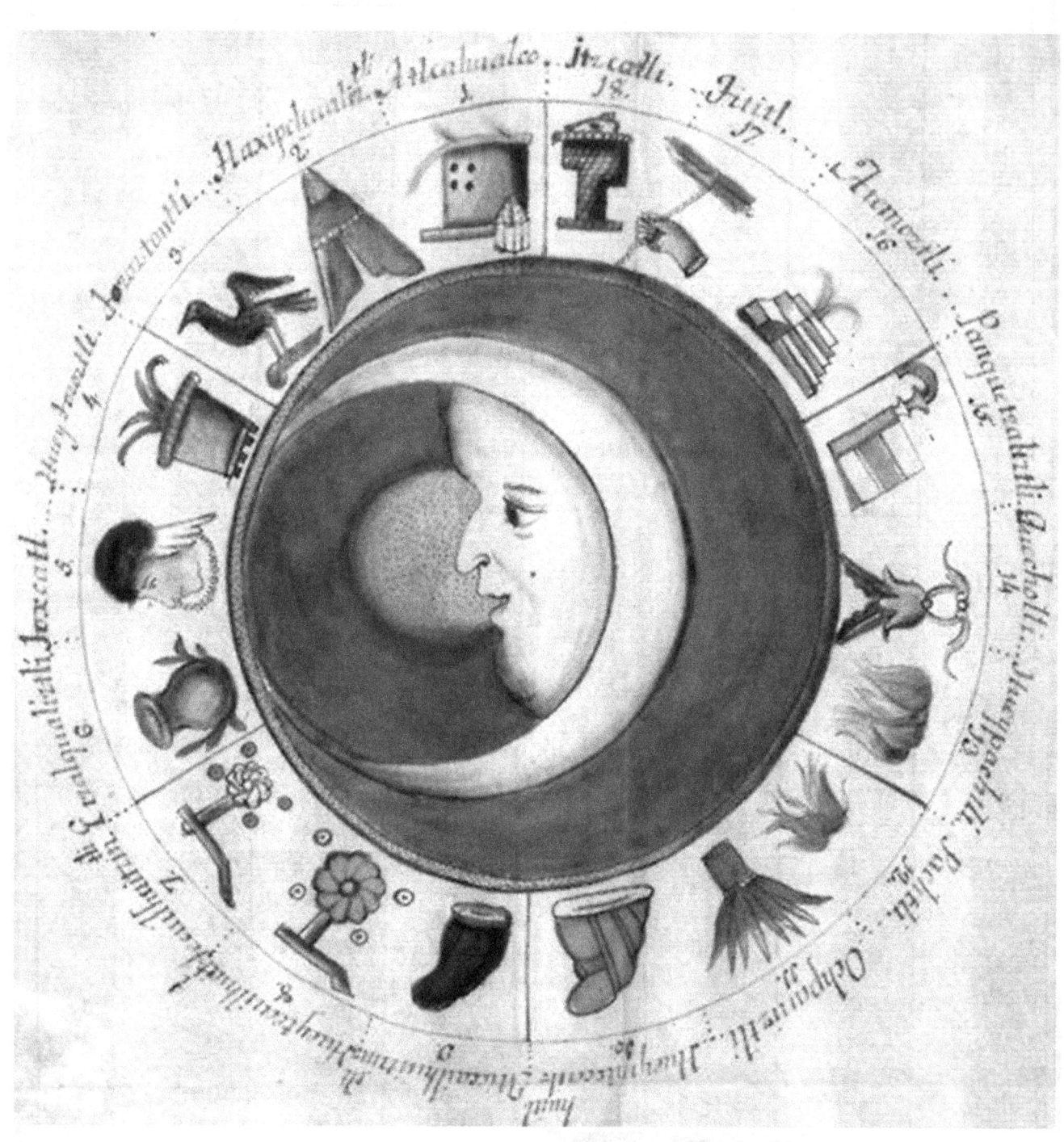

Eliminating Personal Poverty

This spell ensures that you always have the necessities of life, such as somewhere to stay and enough to eat. Because it becomes part of your everyday environment, you simply need to refresh the ingredients when you feel the time right.

You will need the following items for this spell:

    Small glass container containing equal quantities of:

    Salt, sugar and rice

    Safety pin

Fill the container with a mixture of the salt, sugar and rice.

Place the open safety pin in the centre of the mixture.

Put the container in the open air where you can easily see it.

Occasionally give the bowl a shake to reinvigorate the energies. Though this spell has no particular timeframe, the more confident you become in your own abilities the quicker it will work.

Shaking the container also keeps the energies fresh and you must use your intuition as to when they need changing.

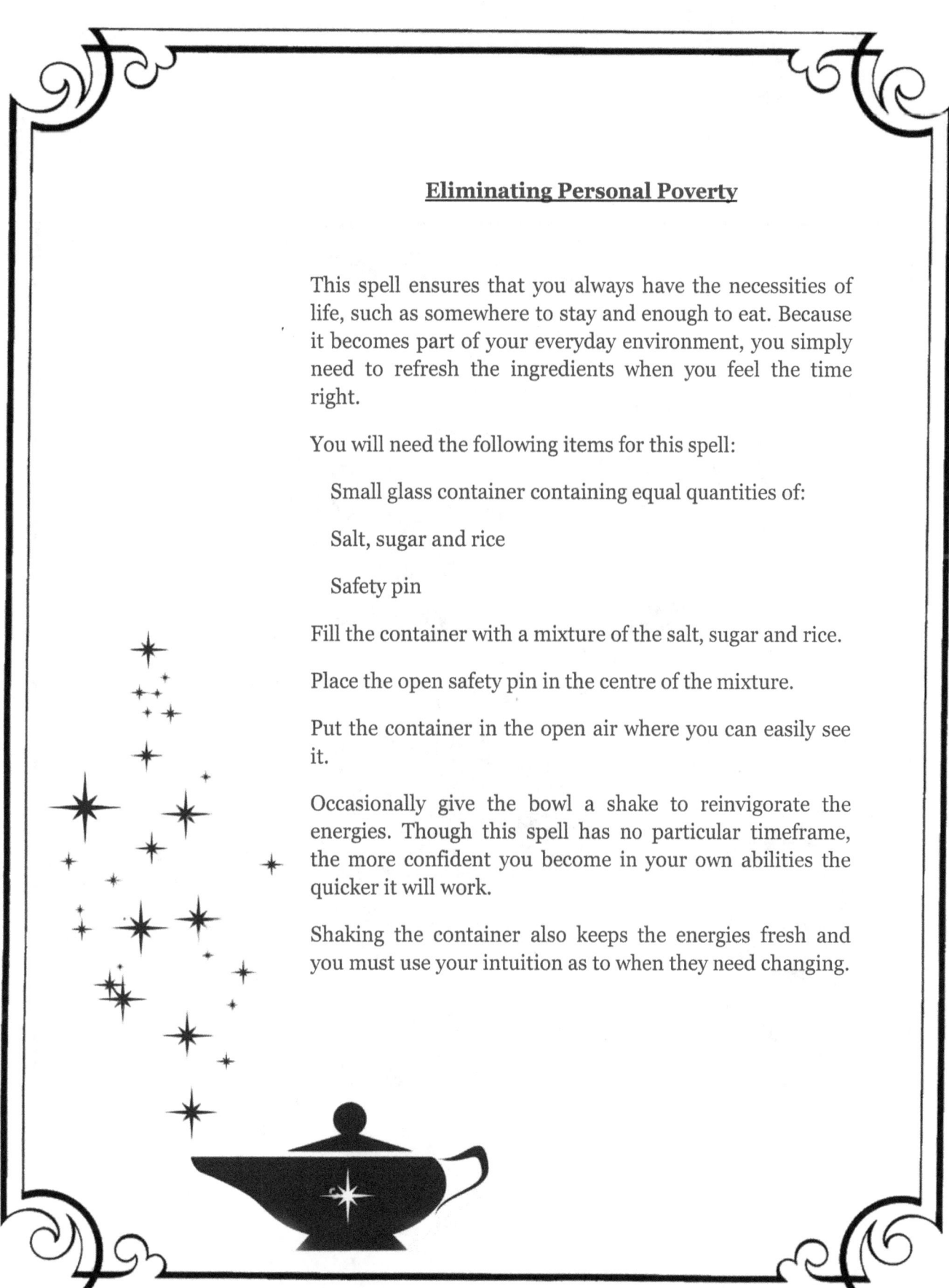

Money Talisman

You will need the following items for this spell:

- Five pumpkinseeds
- Three Cinnamon sticks
- One dollar bill
- Green cloth
- Green candle
- Cinnamon or basil oil
- Green ribbon

On a Friday during the waxing moon, assemble all your ingredients at dusk. Take the candle and rub (Prosperity, basil or cinnamon) oil into it while focusing on your bills and debts being paid, see them being paid, picture yourself writing checks. Light the candle and take the green cloth, add the pumpkinseeds, Cinnamon sticks, and the dollar bill and fold three times, tie with ribbon. Chant while you work and focus on money coming towards you:

Dollar bill, work your will.

Pumpkinseeds do your deeds.

Cinnamon sticks, do the trick,

Bring needed money & bring it quick.

Repeat three times burn candle for nine minutes.

Keep Talisman near your wallet or purse, and bills to be paid.

Expect money to come, know it will and it shall.

<u>Increase Wealth of Household</u>

This spell has the power to increase the wealth of everyone in the household.

You will need the following items for this spell:

Small amount of green paint

Full moon

On an evening the full moon is clearly visible, go outside and under its light paint your index finger with green paint. Go to your doorway and above it place your green. Fingerprint while saying:

Those who pass beneath

Have their personal wealth increased

Your fingerprint can be in an inconspicuous place if you live in someone else's house or apartment. It doesn't have to be obvious unless you want it to be.

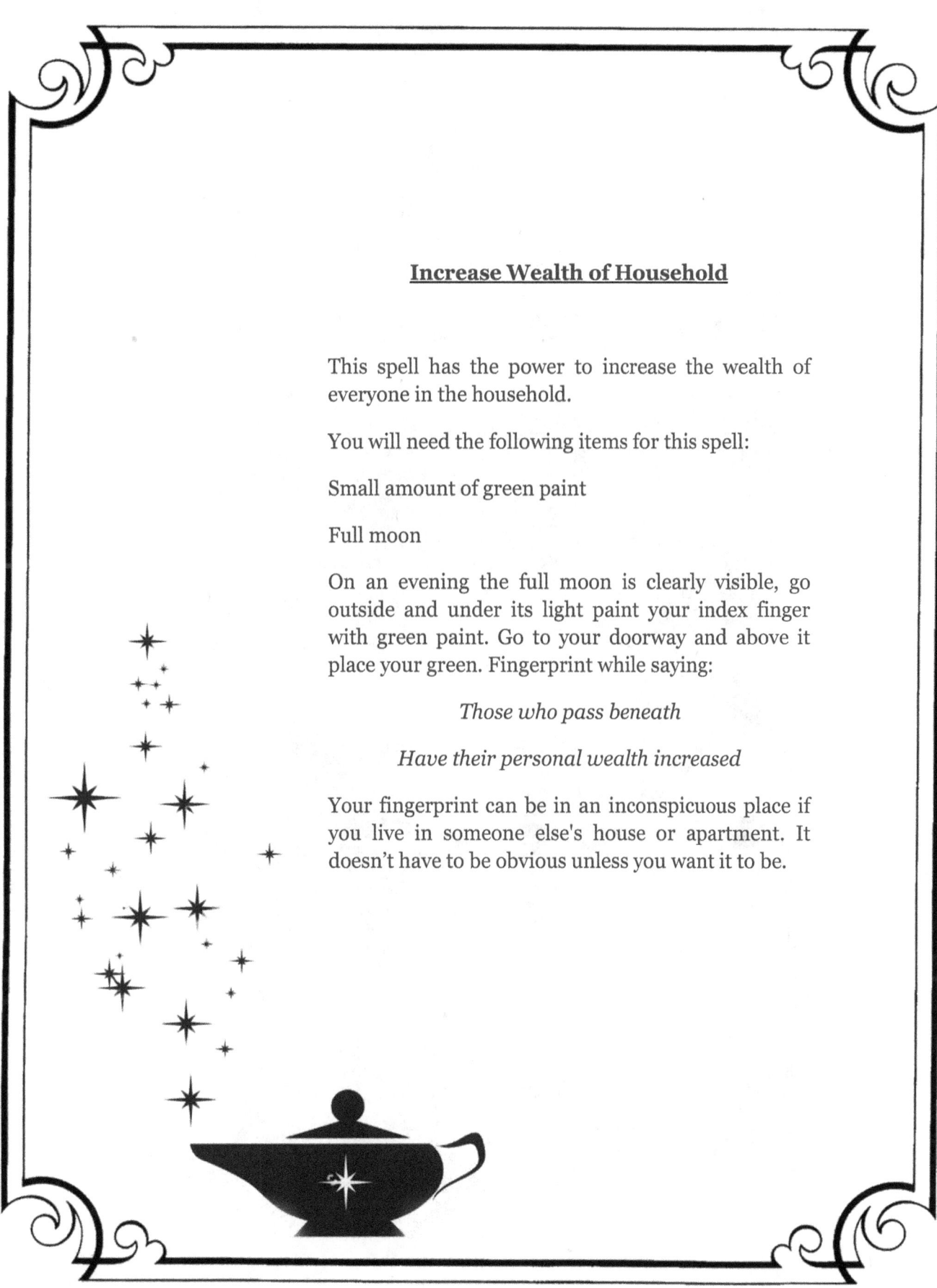

Spells to Banish Health Problems

Write the name of your health problem on a piece of paper and use a permanent marker or white-out to "erase" the name completely.

Write the name of your health problem on a piece of toilet paper and flush it away.

Write the name of your health problem on piece of paper with, and put it through your paper shredder.

Write the name of your health problem on a scrap of old sweater and unravel the yarn.

Carve the name of your health problem on a black candle and let it burn all the way down.

Carve the name of your health problem on a scrap of wood and burn it (Fallen branches are the best choice here, as lumber scraps might be treated with chemicals and plywood contains glue).

Write the name of your health problem on a leaf, river rock or shell and throw it into running water (only throw into the water what came out of it or what might naturally fall into it).

Write the name of your health problem on a piece of paper and burn it in a heat proof container or fire place.

Carve the name of your health problem into the skin of a banana or other fruit and bury it in the earth.

Whisper the words "I banish you, (insert name here) into a soap bubble and let the wind carry it away from you.

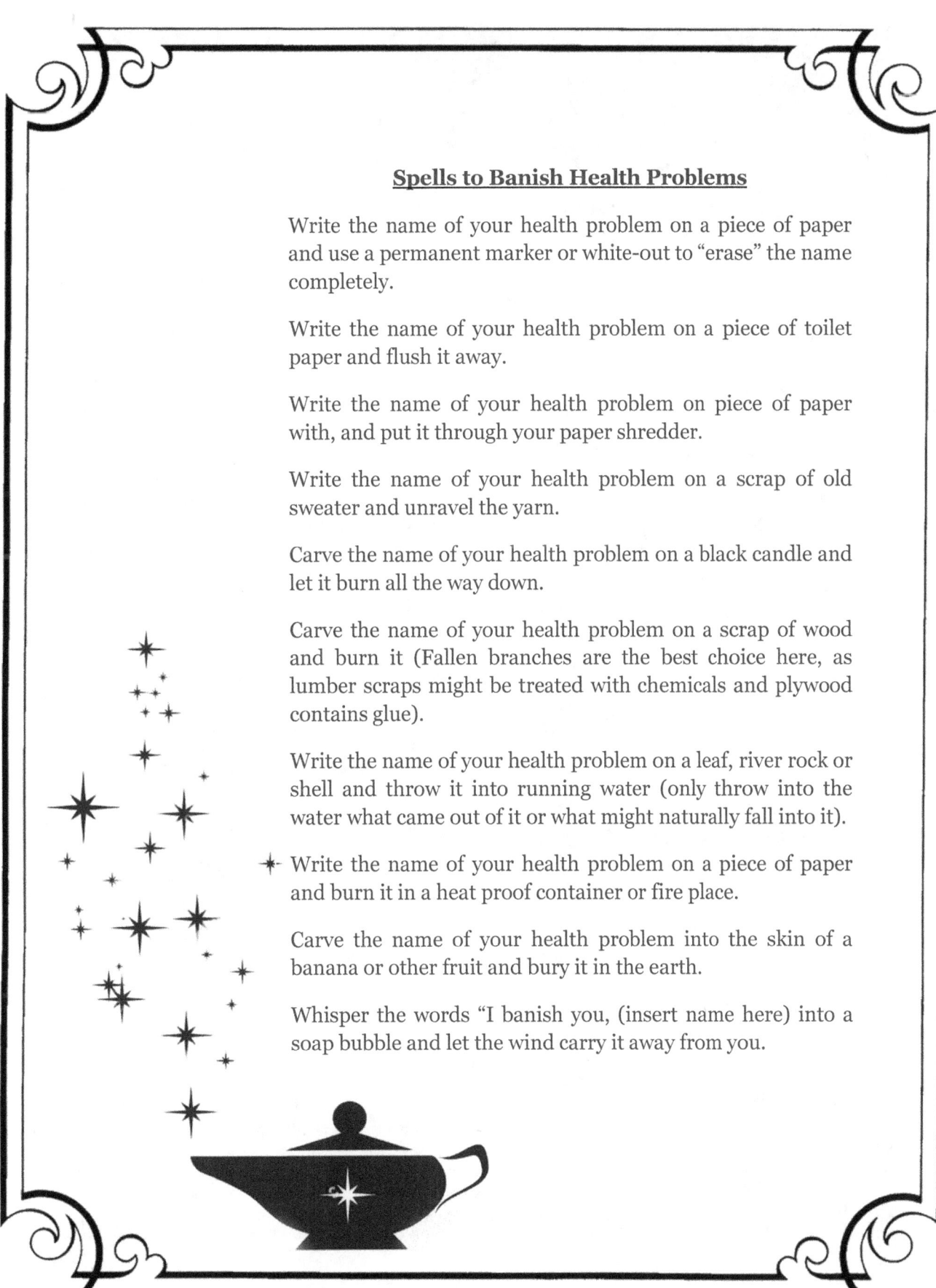

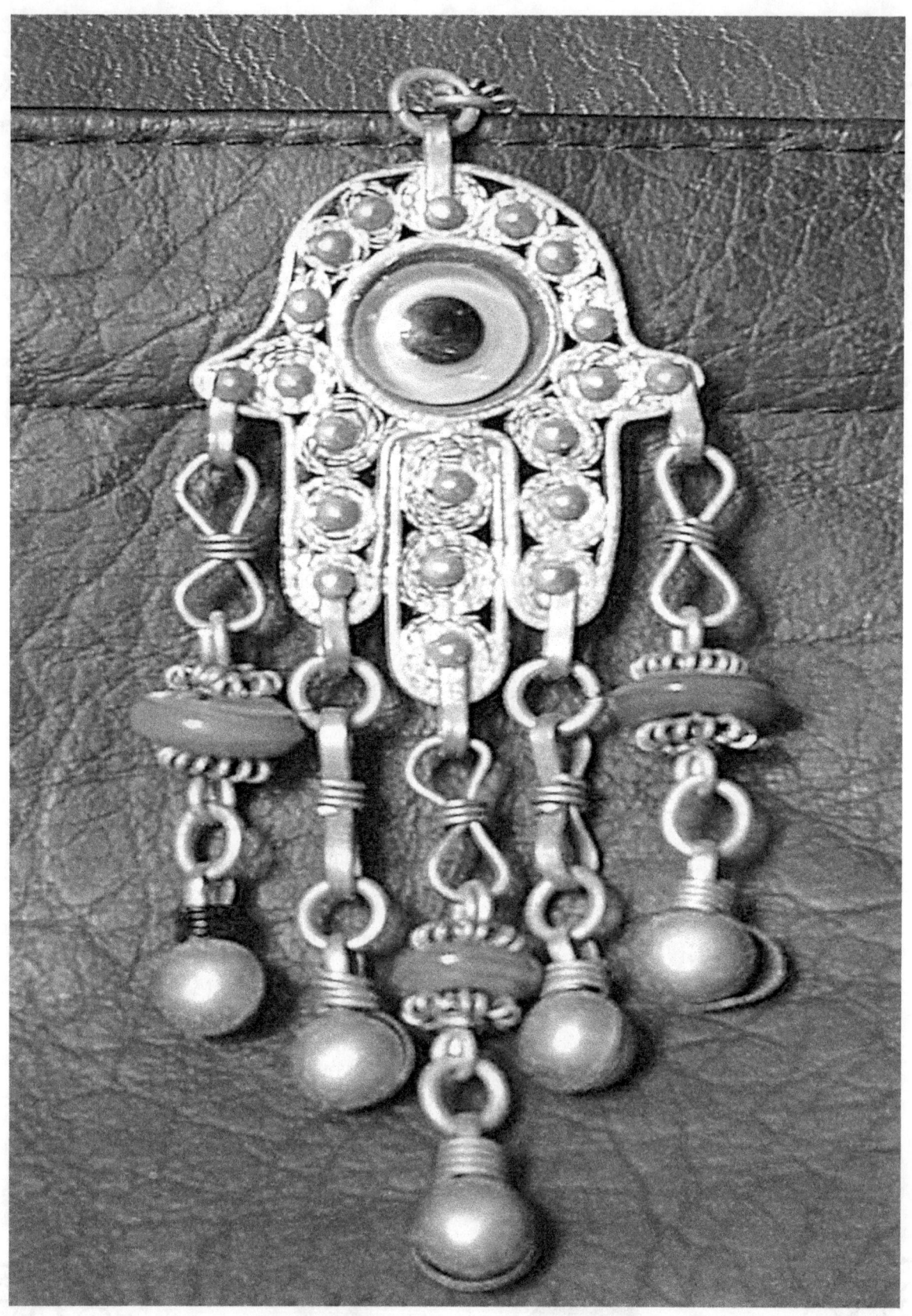

Magickal Days And How to Use Them

This list shows the best days to perform certain Spells or Magickal workings.

Sunday - Sun - Good for Joy, Healing, Hope, Truth, Positive Energy, Business and Friends.

Monday - Moon - Good for Protection in Journeys, Clairvoyance, Intuition, Health of the body, getting rid of Enemies and other Evil things or Beings.

Tuesday - Mars - Good for Strength, Passion, Confidence, and winning Judgment to ones favor.

Wednesday - Mercury - Good for Divination, Dreams, preventing Poverty, and for attaining Knowledge of thing of this World and the Spirits World.

Thursday - Jupiter - Good for Money, Riches and favor, Peace, Love, Concord, appeasing Enemies and confirming Honors and Dignities.

Friday - Venus - Love, Passion, Sex, Conception, ending Strife, dissolving Enchantments and promoting Concord.

Saturday - Saturn - Good for Past Life Recall, Illness, Bindings and Banishings or getting rid of Negative Energies or Bad Habits.

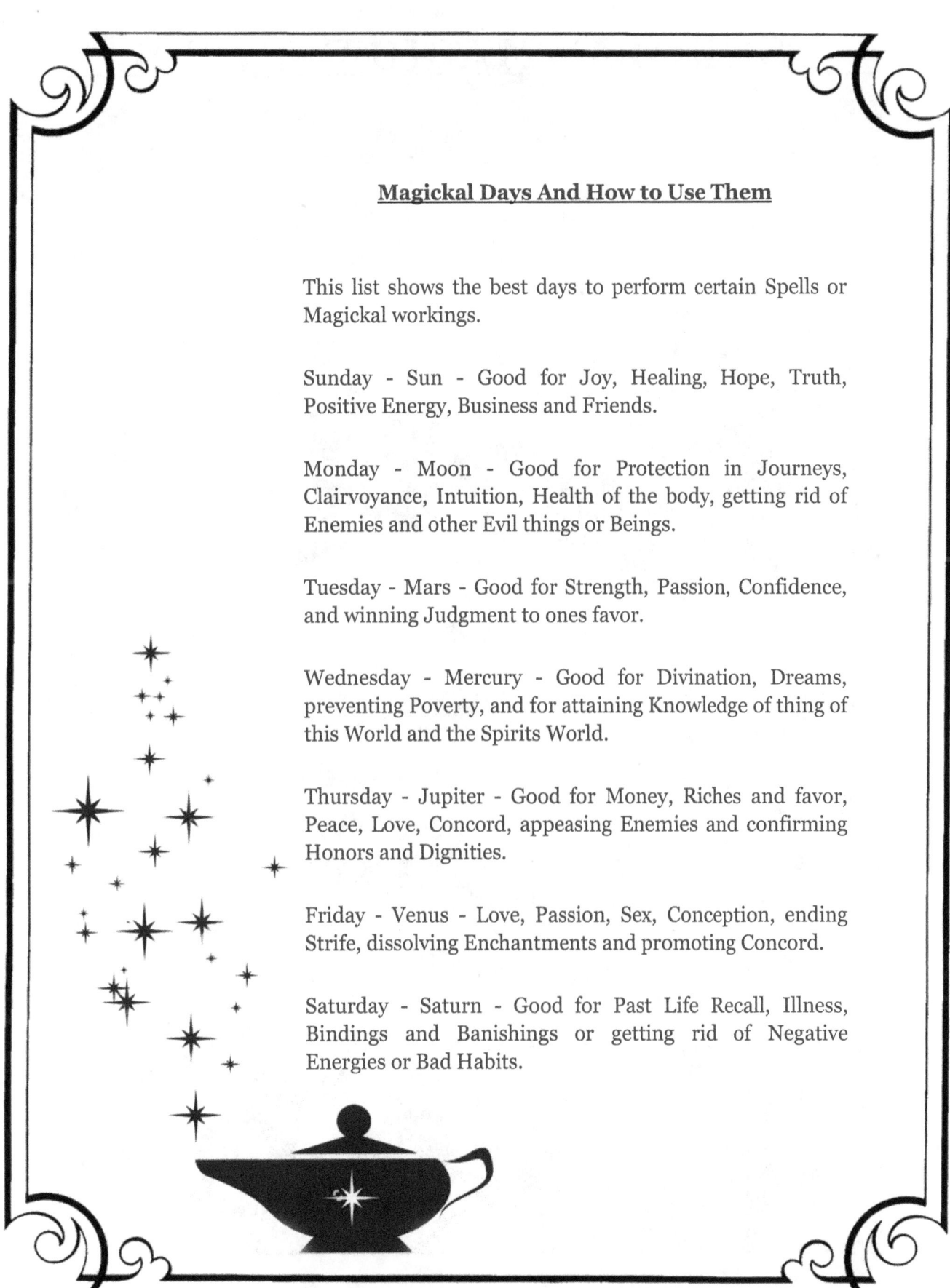

SCHOLÆ MAGICÆ TYPVS

Mons Magorum Invisibilis

Regio Phantastica

Lumen Naturæ

Thesaurus Incantatus

Non nisi Parvulis

Unlucky Days

According to the Ancients, the following days are considered to be unlucky. It is best not to get involved in a relationship, get married, start a new business, buy a house or car, or any type of new activities on these days:

January 1, 2, 6, 14, 27

February 1, 17, 19

March 11, 26

April 10, 27, 28

May 11, 12

June 19 July 18, 21

August 2, 26, 27

September 10, 18

October 6

November 6, 17

December 5, 14, 23

Healing Flames

Draw a picture of yourself with the disease, wound or condition.

Clearly point out the problem in the picture: a large hammer against the head to represent a headache; black worms for a virus; a broken limb; a sore.

Charge a red candle with healing energy. Light the candle's flame.

Hold the tip of the picture in the flame. After it's lit, drop it into a heat proof container.

Now, with the red candle still burning, draw another picture of yourself without the headache, free of the virus or sore, or with a healed limb.

Place this picture under the red candle & let it burn out.

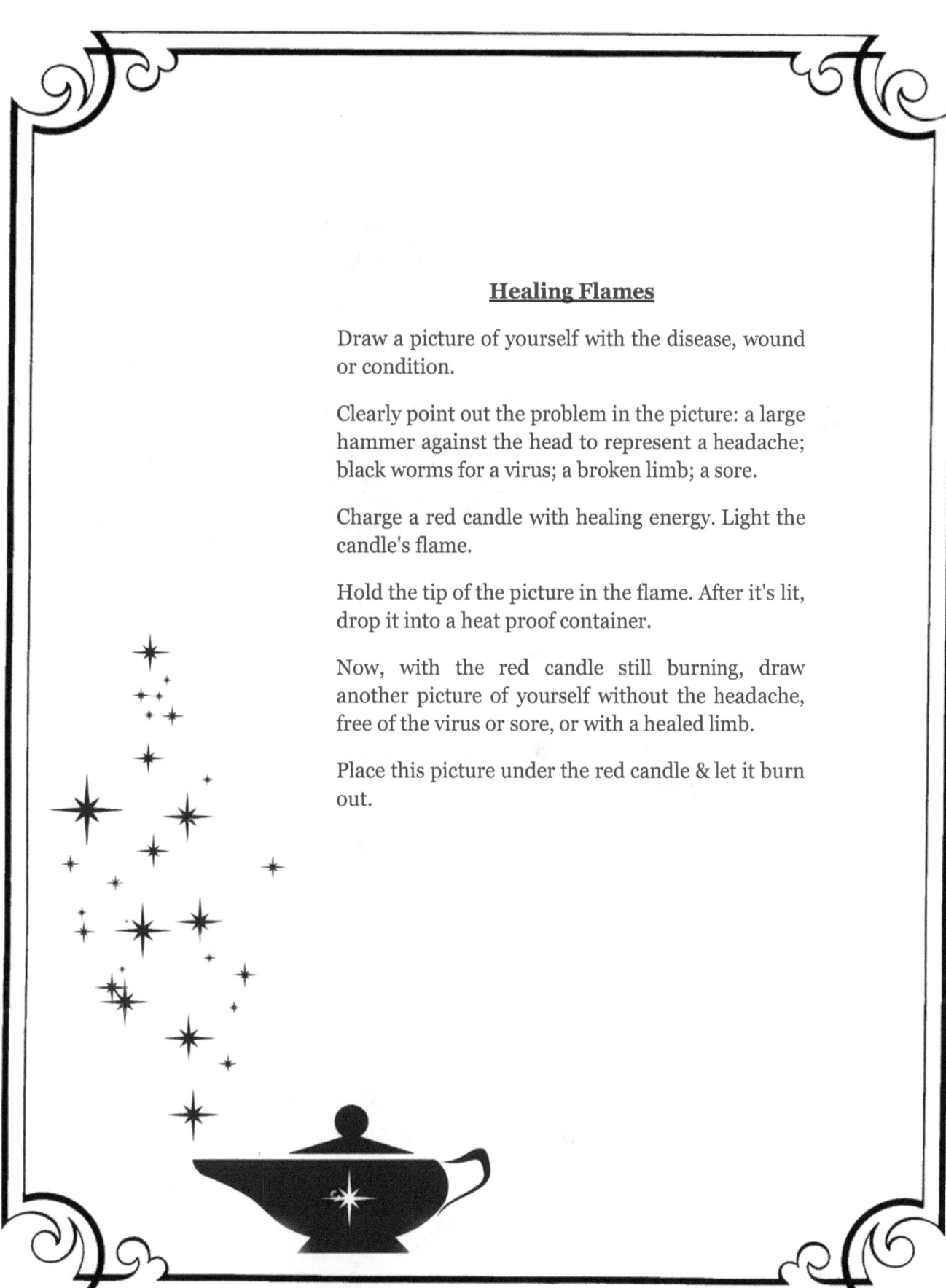

Omens of Good Luck

If a spider drops in front of you it is good luck, or expect good news very soon.

If one dreams of pulling in a flying kite, they will soon fall heir to a large fortune.

To be completely naked in your dream is a very lucky omen. If only your feet are bare, you will have many difficulties to overcome before you can reach your goal.

To dream of someone smoking a cigar indicates that money is on its way.

If you involuntarily make a rhyme, that is a lucky omen. Before speaking again, make a wish, and the chances are that it will come true.

It is a sign of good luck if you first see the new moon over your left shoulder, but of bad luck if you see it over your right.

Should you have money in your pocket at the time of the new moon, you will be penniless before the moon is in the full.

To sneeze three times in rapid succession is considered by some to be a good omen.

To Be Blessed At All Times

To be assured of God's blessing every day, say this silently to yourself in the morning upon arising from bed:

I conjure thee, sword, sabre or knife, that mightest injure or harm me, by the priest of all prayers, who had gone into the temple at Jerusalem, and said: An edged sword shall pierce your soul that you may not injure me, who am a child of God.

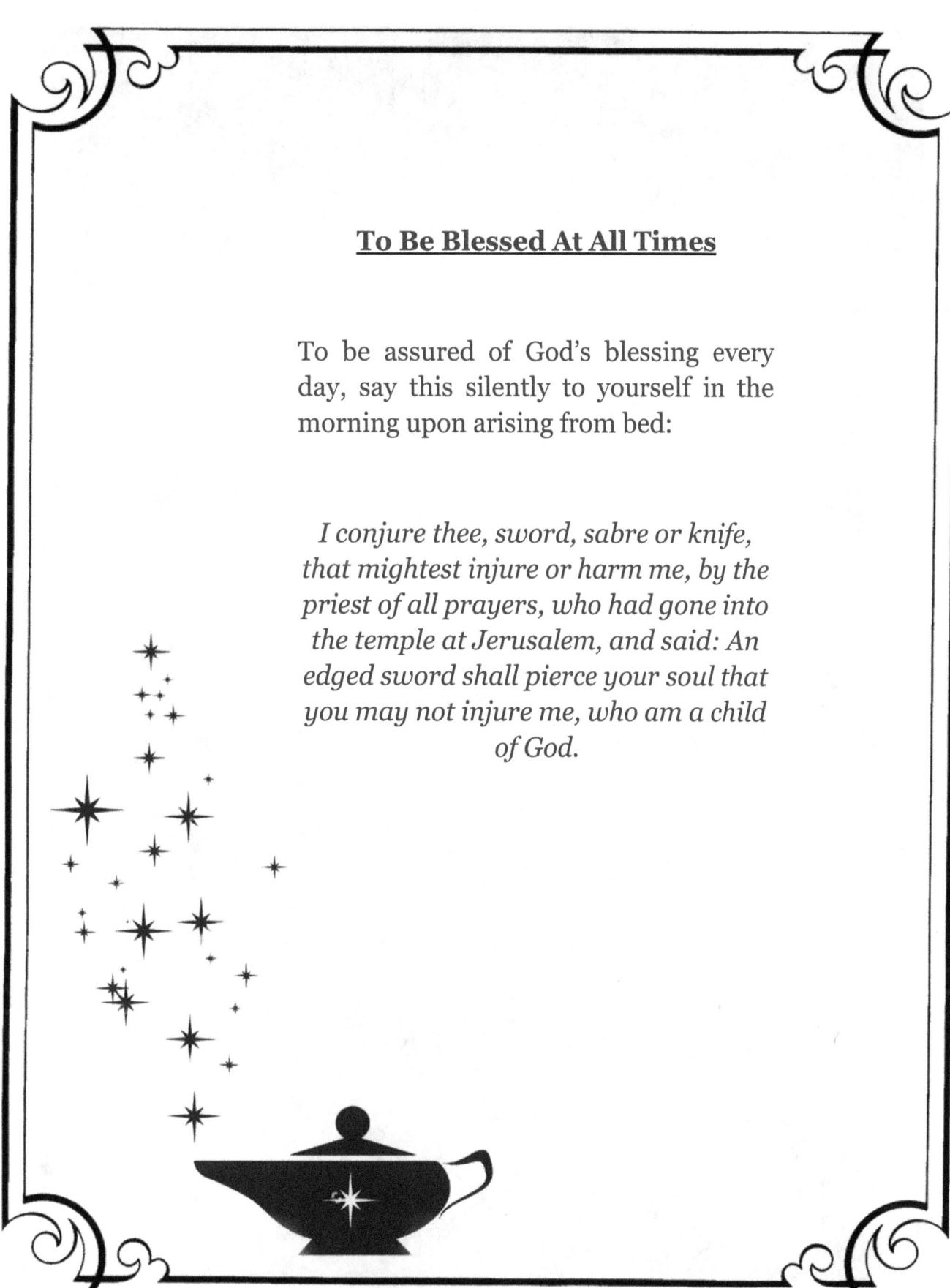

Charm Against Trouble in General

Repeat reverently, and with sincere faith, the following words, and you shall be protected in the hour of danger:

He shall deliver thee in six troubles, yea, in seven there shall no evil touch thee; in famine he shall redeem thee from death, and in war from the power of the sword; and thou shall know that thy tabernacle shall be in peace, and thou shalt visit thy habitation and shall not err.

Maria D' Andrea

If you enjoyed this book, please drop us a line for your FREE catalog of our fine collection of books, videos and other interesting items!

Send Your Name and Mailing Address to:

Global Communications

P.O. Box 753

New Brunswick, NJ 08903

Email: mrufo8@hotmail.com

www.conspiracyjournal.com

SPELLCRAFT, WISECRAFT, OCCULT, METAPHYSICS
Workbooks And Study Guides From Qualified Instructors

MARIA D' ANDREA

Maria is a gifted psychic, spiritual counselor, and shaman. She has helped those in matters of luck, love and financial concerns. She lectures, holds workshops and does private counseling in NY area. Her books are exclusively published by Tim Beckley.

HEAVEN SENT MONEY SPELLS
IMAGINE RECEIVING MONEY JUST BY USING THE POWERS OF YOUR MIND! Let Maria D' Andrea Tell You How To Turn Your Dreams Into Cash — And Become A Virtual Human MONEY MAGNET. Inspired by the Heavenly Light. Here are spells that anyone can learn to execute. Use herbs, candles and gemstones to create prosperity! Have talismans and amulets help do the work for you!
8.5x11—Workbook format—132 pages—ISBN-13: 978-1606111000—$19.95

SECRET OCCULT GALLERY AND SPELL CASTING FORMULARY
COME UP TO THE "GOOD LIFE" with Maria's top dozen enchantments and occult gallery of mystical and spiritual essentials. Easy to perform spells that could put you on easy street.
8.5x11—Workbook format—152 pages—ISBN-13: 978-1606111284—$21.95

YOUR PERSONAL MEGA POWER SPELLS
A valuable interpretation of blessings, protections, hex-breaking rituals and ceremonies as practiced by the most ardent of Wiccans, alchemists, sages and occultists down through the centuries.
8.5X11—252 pages—ISBN-13: 978-1606111055—$21.95

SECRET MAGICAL ELIXIRS OF LIFE
Explore The Paranormal Vibrations Of Crystals, Gems And Stones For Good Health, Enhanced Psychic Powers And Phenomenal Inner Strength!
8.5X11—150 PAGES—ISBN-13: 978-1606111147—$21.95

HOW TO ELIMINATE ANXIETY AND STRESS THROUGH THE OCCULT
Just utilize Crystals, Gemstones, Meditation, Herbs, Oils, Visualization, Chakras, Music, Prayer, Mandalas, Mantras, Incense, Candles and More.
6x9—150 pages—ISBN-13: 978-1606111383—$19.95

MYSTICAL, MAGICKAL BEASTS AND BEINGS
Come explore the supernatural side of man's best – and worst – "friends" as related in the strangest stories involving beasties of all sorts – seen and unseen. And uppermost learn how to get them to assist in our lives in a positive way. Other contributors include Penny Melis and Sean Casteel.
8.5x11—224 pages—ISBN-13: 978-1606111567—$21.95

OCCULT GRIMORIE AND MAGICAL FORMULARY
10 BOOKS ROLLED INTO ONE! – OVER 500 SPELLS! Reveals the secret of the ages. Manifest your destiny NOW! Most powerful spellcasters deliberately leave out important information. NOT MARIA!
8.5x11—236 pages—ISBN-13: 978-1606111086—$24.00

SUPER SPECIAL: Retail customers get all of Maria's books as listed for $139.00 + $15.00 Postage/Shipping. FREE DVD WITH 3 OF MARIA'S BOOKS OR MORE

SUBSCRIBE TO OUR YOUTUBE CHANNEL — MR UFOS SECRET FILES

SOMETHING DIFFERENT – A REFRESTING CHANGE
A BEAUTIFUL LARGE FORMAT "COFFEE TABLE" BOOK
PROFUSELY ILLUSTRATED

SPOOKY TREASURE TROVES
UFOS, GHOSTS, CURSED PIECES OF EIGHT AND THE PARANORMAL

Everyone has fantasized about finding buried treasure. Its a child's dream and many a grown person's obsession. Thousands own metal detectors and regularly scan the shore line, creek beds and out of the way mountain crevices looking for that proverbial treasure trove.

SPOOKY TREASURE TROVES offers the reader both escapism and possibly a rare opportunity to unlock the key to discovering some fabulous fortune that has lain hidden away for decades, perhaps even centuries. Join Tim Beckley, Sean Casteel, Paul Eno, Dr. Nandor Fodor, Scott Corralles, Preston Dennett and Paul Dale Roberts as they provide guidance in searching for a million dollars or more in gold, diamonds, rare doubloons or old art masterpieces.

But above all else you will learn of the "supernatural treasure hunting connection" that includes the appearance of UFOs, ghosts, spirits of deceased Native Americans and even Bigfoot who are either guarding vast treasures or have been known to lead deserving souls to the end of a rainbow.

For example, the late "UFO prophet" Ted Owens recounts conducting a séance at a hotel in Durago, Mexico where he sought to recover a hidden treasure. – ** Renowned psychoanalyst and parapsychologist Dr. Nandor Fodor offers his expertise on the mysteries surrounding a treasure of 55 million dollars on a Central American island and the uncanny supernatural presence that hovers around it. – ** Writer Sean Casteel reports on eerie happenings on a mountain in Oregon, where it is said a slave's ghost guards over the treasure of the pirates who killed him. – ** Meanwhile, UFOs guard Viking treasure in Greenland, and the ghost of an Old West outlaw silently points toward his buried, ill-gotten gains. – ** And the well known and prolific Scott Corrales provides stories of supernatural guardians of treasure that stretch from South America to Lebanon. – ** There is also Preston Dennett's experiences with "spook lights," as well as Tim and Charla's encounter with the ghosts of Jerome, AZ, and the famous Phoenix Lights and their possible connection with the Lost Dutchman Mine. – ** And let's not forget the curse of Oak Island, where the money pit has been responsible for the deaths of several treasure hunters (not many buffs realize UFOs have been sighted and ghostly figures encountered on this wind swept parcel of land off the coast of Nova Scotia.).

Shiver me timbers its all here – and a heck of a lot more, my matey. Order SPOOKY TREASURE TROVES (regular price - $29.00) for just $25.00 + $7 S/H – ('cause its so huge).

TIMOTHY G BECKLEY, BOX 753, NEW BRUNSWICK, NJ 08903

Listen Live Thursday's at 7 PM Pacific / 10 PM Eastern at KCORradio.com – Fabulous Guests. Now archived on KCOR Digital Radio and on Mr UFOs Secret Files on YouTube

NOW AVAILABLE!
THE FABULOUS MONEY MAGNET KIT
Triple Strength Good Luck Charm Can Make You An Instant Winner!!!
MONEY MAGNET & SUPER SPELL KIT
We supply the blessings and the money activating amulet and every thing you need to work your money magic spell.
Just $22 + $5 S/H
Actual Items May Vary From Art
ORDER FROM: TIMOTHY G BECKLEY
BOX 753, NEW BRUNSWICK, NJ 08903
732 602-3407 mrufo8@hotmail.com (PayPal Orders Fastest0

WATCH AND SUBSCRIBE TO OUR FREE YOUTUBE CHANNEL—MR UFOS SECRET FILES

Updated Edition!
SECRETS OF THE REAL DOCTOR FRANKENSTEIN
Mad Scientist
Andrew Crosse— Monster Maker

Did he create the building blocks of life in his laboratory? Or was he delusional? Or perhaps even a total fraud? His contemporaries in the scientific community were puzzled by the very nature of his experiments. And while the eye does not deceive, they were unable to duplicate his findings and reproduce under controlled conditions the striking life forms that were plainly visible and clearly moving around Crosse's laboratory table.

To the farmers living in the area surrounding Crosse's palatial Fyne Court, he quickly became recognized as a heretic dabbling in dark areas that led him to be on the receiving end of a significant number of irate letters from God-fearing folk who summarily and loudly accused him of blasphemy, or even trying to replace their God as the ultimate creator.

The contentions of the nearby country folk were only compounded by Andrew Crosse's ability to seemingly capture bolts of lightning and direct them through a mile long coil of copper wire that was suspended from poles and trees all around his estate. Events reached a boiling point when Crosse began to receive anonymous death threats. There were those who firmly blamed him for a failure in the year's wheat-crop; and there was even a demand that an exorcism of the whole area be undertaken in the surrounding green hills. It is said that the author of Frankenstein, Mary Shelly, got her inspiration from Crosse's "demented" laboratory experiments.

Order: Secrets of Dr Frankenstein – $22.00
Large Format - 350 Pages—ISBN: 16061111906
Timothy Green Beckley Box 753 · New Brunswick, NJ 08903

SPECIAL – THREE BOOKS—*The Bell Witch, Mad Mollie and Secrets Of The Real Doctor Frankenstein— 49.00 + $5.00 S/H (SEE THE NEXT PAGE)*

DARE YOU FIND THE TRUTH ABOUT?..
America's Strange And Supernatural History:
Includes: Prophecies Of The Presidents

No one would likely dispute the fact that times are stranger in America than ever, and indications are things are getting weirder with each passing day. But a look at our hidden – SECRET – history alerts us to the startling fact that our country has been steeped in "high strangeness" since the Declaration of Independence was signed. It is apparent that our proud nation owes a great "debt of gratitude" to the mysterious, the macabre, the downright bizarre unseen realm of the occult.

** – Did the Lemurians, a Pacific Ocean race similar to the fabled Atlanteans to the east, erect the mysterious walls found in the eastern part of the San Francisco Bay area? **Writer Olav Phillips** explores the enigma first hand.

** – **Sean Casteel** provides an overview of historical incidents of cannibalism, stories that go back as far as "The Starving Time" of the Jamestown colony in 1609.

** – **William Michael Mott** offers up some of the UFO and creature sightings he has collected from the state of Mississippi – going way back.

** – Publisher/writer **Timothy Green Beckley** and his friend **Circe** returned to Sleepy Hollow, New York – of "Headless Horseman" fame – and discovered that paranormal activity is still rampant there.

** — Author **Tim Swartz** would like suitable explanations for all the supernatural mysteries of his native Indiana, including lake monsters, Bigfoot sightings, anomalous big cats, UFOs and more. As well as the the "demon gasser" of Mattoon, Illinois who did his best to contaminate several small communities.

In a Bonus Section: "The Spiritual Destiny of America" - The future of America as seen through the eyes of prophecy and the occult is revealed. You can feel the chills already, eh?

Order: AMERICA'S STRANGE AND SUPERNATURAL HISTORY
for just $20.00 + $5 S/H
and get ready to kick those chills up a notch or two.

ON LINE AT www.ConspiracyJournal.com AND www.TeslaSecretLab.com

ONCE BELIEVED TO BE ONLY FOR THE "PRIVILEGED," HERE IS ARCANE KNOWLEDGE PASSED DOWN THROUGH THE CENTURIES

NOW FOR THE FIRST TIME YOU CAN TAKE ADVANTAGE OF THESE THREE INCREDIBLY INSPIRED STUDY GUIDES FOR YOUR OWN PERSONAL BENEFIT

1 – THE PYRAMIDS SPEAK

This work includes ten of the most magical good luck talismans and amulets from the powerful high priests of Ancient Egypt. Here are antediluvian mysteries and controversial knowledge, as adapted from the Pharaohs and Shamans who lived along the Nile, which remain of great benefit to mankind even today and which you can use yourself as if you were turning back the hands of time. And while the pyramids have often been associated with the mummification of royal remains, the truth is that the pyramids were not really intended to be tombs.

MANY QUESTIONS ANSWERED TO BENEFIT ALL!

** Does A Time Capsule Rest Under The Great Pyramid? – ** Will The Cross Jesus Was Crucified On Be Found Beneath The Sands of Egypt? – ** Did Spaceships Use The Pyramids To Recharge So They Could Return Home? – ** Did The Ancients Realize That The Shape of The Pyramid Itself Was Very Powerful? – ** Why Has The Fact That Pyramids Have Been Found All Over The Planet Been Withheld From The Public?

FREE BONUS – BOOK ABOVE CONTAINS A MINATURE PYRAMID "KIT" TO COPY WHICH IS BELIEVED TO HAVE MAGICAL POWERS YOU CAN TAP INTO ON YOUR OWN – PUT IT TOGETHER AND COUNT TO THREE!

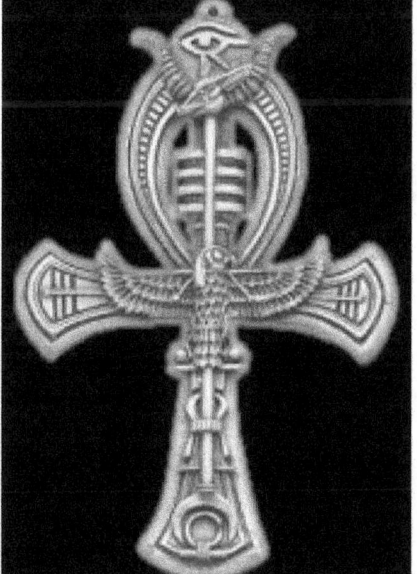

2 – SECRETS OF EGYPTIAN SPELLCASTING

Moses is said to have followed in the footsteps of the great Egyptians and adapted their magical formulas. Now you can unlock the occult wisdom of antiquity and experience the awesome miracle of Egyptian magic, known to be the most powerful of all time! From the records of the prestigious "Keeper of the Egyptian and Assyrian Antiquities" (circa 1895) at the British Museum comes long forgotten knowledge of how to make use of dreams, tap the power of lucky and unlucky days, and utilize talismans and charms initially designed in the distant past and still useful and beneficial today.

Every man, woman and child in ancient Egypt who could afford it wore either a charm or talisman, and for centuries their land was regarded as a nation of powerful magicians and sorcerers who guided their citizens in all matters mystical and spiritual. Hebrew, Greek and Roman writers referred to them as experts in the occult sciences and as possessors of arcane wisdom and knowledge which could, according to the given circumstances, be employed to do either good or harm to man. Here are the actual spells and formulas utilized by the wizards of this ancient paradise along the Nile, as well as the designs of their most powerful amulets and talismans that have made Egyptian Magic the most commanding form of occultism ever performed at any time during the history of humankind.

3 – TAROSTAR'S (ANCIENT) BOOK OF SHADOWS

Used for centuries by members of the Craft, here are dozens of unique spells, including Six Days For Money, To Cast The Money Circle, Candle in The Grave, Jinx Removing And Reversing. A genuine working record of Craft rituals and spells. This grimoire is a detailed manual for any practitioner of witchcraft. In addition to the multitude of spells, divination techniques, and procedures to reverse hexes/curses, this tome focuses on ritual practices for the small coven. Included are basic instructions on how to conduct ritual, as well as detailed examples of ceremonial procedures for various occasions and rituals for all eight Sabbaths. Combined with the use of incense and candles, this book of wisdom can be easily applied by those serious about their spiritual work.

All Books Are Set In Large Easy To Read Format – $20 EACH – Special 3 Book Set $54 +$6 S/H

TIMOTHY GREEN BECKLEY
BOX 753, NEW BRUNSWICK, NJ 08903

www.ingramcontent.com/pod-product-compliance
Lightning Source LLC
Chambersburg PA
CBHW080514110426
42742CB00017B/3112